ERICAS
OF THE FYNBOS

John Manning & Nick Helme
with Ross Turner

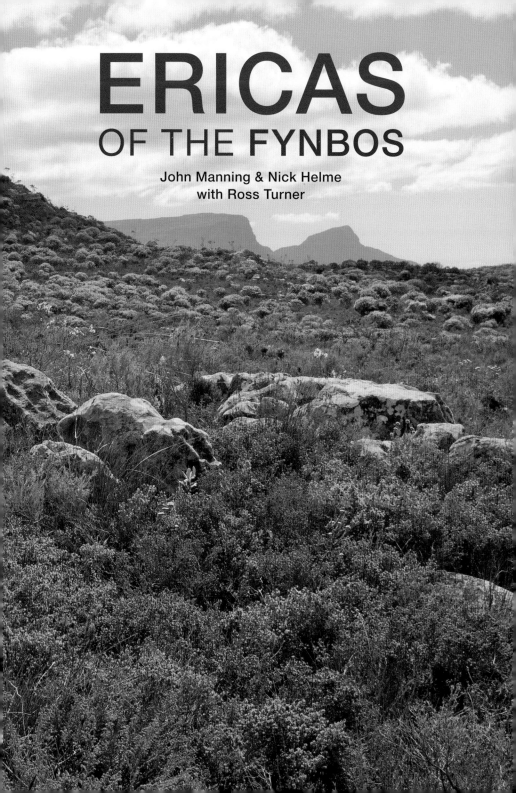

ERICAS
OF THE FYNBOS

John Manning & Nick Helme
with Ross Turner

ACKNOWLEDGEMENTS

We are grateful to all the iNaturalist contributors who responded so enthusiastically to our request for images; Dee Paterson-Jones for her interest and for providing several fine images from the Colin Paterson-Jones Archive; Elizabeth Parker, Jakes Wallage and Corinne Merry for their willing support in the field; Ross Turner for additional images and for generously offering us the benefit of his extensive knowledge of Cape ericas; pollen specialist Saúl Manzano for preparing the pollen micrographs especially for this book; and Roelien Theron, Gillian Black and Helen de Villiers for their superb realisation of this guide.

Mapula
Trust

The Publisher extends grateful thanks to the Mapula Trust for its support of this publication.

Published by Struik Nature
(an imprint of Penguin Random House South Africa (Pty) Ltd)
Reg. No. 1953/000441/07
The Estuaries No. 4, Oxbow Crescent, Century Avenue, Century City, 7441
PO Box 1144, Cape Town, 8000 South Africa

Visit **www.struiknature.co.za** and join the Struik Nature Club for updates, news, events and special offers.

First published in 2024
10 9 8 7 6 5 4 3 2 1

Publisher: Pippa Parker
Managing editor: Roelien Theron
Editor: Helen de Villiers
Concept designer: Janice Evans
Designer: Gillian Black
Proofreader: Emsie du Plessis

Reproduction by Studio Repro
Printed and bound in China by Golden Prosperity Printing & Packaging (Heyuan) Co., Ltd

MIX
Paper | Supporting responsible forestry
FSC
www.fsc.org
FSC® C146541

Half-title page: *Erica diaphana* (Peter Thompson)
Title page: Ericas, Cape Peninsula (Colin Paterson-Jones)
Opposite page: *Erica lanata* (Nicky van Berkel)
Back cover: *Erica discolor* (Ross Turner)

CONTENTS

6

INTRODUCTION

Ericas or heaths, along with proteas and reeds, are one of the distinctive botanical components of the Cape fynbos shrublands that grow at the southwestern tip of Africa. A little under 700 different kinds of ericas are found there, making it easily the most diverse group of plants in the Cape Floristic Region. This is an exceptional diversity when one considers that the next largest genus in the region, *Aspalathus* in the Pea family, has fewer than half this number of species. Ecological studies in the Cape of Good Hope section of Table Mountain National Park have recorded up to 10 different ericas in a single 50m^2 plot, and it is not unusual to find several different ericas growing together in favourable habitats in the mountains of the Western Cape.

What are ericas?

Ericas are evergreen, small-leaved shrubs classified by botanists in the genus *Erica*. They give their name to the large plant family Ericaceae, which includes familiar garden plants such as rhododendrons and azaleas, as well as the popular fruits blueberries and cranberries. Most ericas are low shrubs but some grow into large bushes or small trees. They are generally single-stemmed plants that reproduce solely from seeds since the adult plants are prone to be killed by fire. A few species, however (including some of the more widespread ones), respond positively to periodic burning by coppicing or resprouting multiple stems from a woody rootstock. Most unusually, a few species contain both reseeding and resprouting forms.

PARTS OF AN ERICA PLANT

- **Leaves:** The leaves of ericas are typically small, leathery and usually very narrow or needle-like, and are mostly arranged in close-set whorls.
- **Flowers:** The flowers have 4 sepals and a 4-lobed, more or less bell-shaped or cylindrical corolla (whorl of petals). Most ericas have 8 stamens but a number of the smaller-flowered species have just 4 stamens. These species were formerly included in various other smaller or 'minor' genera and are still known informally as 'minors'. Erica flowers are long-lived and the dried flowers remain on the plants, enclosing the developing fruits.
- **Fruit:** Most erica plants have small, dry fruits that open to release the seeds. The seeds are periodically shed when the plants are shaken, typically by gusts of wind.
- **Seeds:** The seeds are minute and easily dispersed by wind. Depending on the species, some 20,000 to 50,000 erica seeds together can weigh just 1 gram!

The woody lobes or chambers of the fruit split open to release the seed, as seen in *Erica baueri*.

Early botanists defined the genus *Erica* more narrowly than we do today. At that time, true ericas included only those species that had eight stamens and an ovary that was divided internally into four or more compartments. This still amounts to over 700 species, of which some 500 are South African. The remaining heath species were dispersed among more than 20 smaller genera, based on minute floral differences. These genera were known collectively as the smaller or minor genera. They have since been united with *Erica*, largely through the work of the erica specialists Ted and Inge Oliver, but the species that were placed in them are still known informally as 'minors'. Most of the minors are easily recognised by having just four anthers, often protruding from the mouth of the flower. They number a little over 100 species in South Africa, mainly in the Cape Floristic Region, with a few dozen others in tropical Africa and Madagascar.

Although tremendous variation occurs in the *Erica* genus, all species share the same features, as illustrated here in *Erica plukenetii* subsp. *plukenetii* and *Erica scytophylla* (inset).

HEATHER VS HEATH

Confusingly, the term **heather** is frequently misapplied to heaths, or ericas. True heather is a similar and related species belonging to the genus *Calluna*, whereas heaths are members of the genus *Erica*. The Common Heather, or Ling, *Calluna vulgaris*, is the sole species of heather and occurs naturally in Europe and Asia Minor as the dominant plant in most heathlands and moorlands, and in some bog vegetation and acidic pine and oak woodlands. It is the iconic heather of Scotland.

ihorhvozdetskiy/AdobeStock

A Common Heather heathland. Heather differs from ericas by having stalkless leaves.

ADAPTIVE TRAITS OF LEAVES

A key ecological adaptation of ericas lies in the structure of their leaves. The small, leathery leaves are sealed on the outside by a thick wax layer or *cuticle* that prevents moisture loss from the surface. In addition, the margins of the leaves are rolled under so that only a narrow strip of

A narrow groove in the leaves encloses the stomata or 'breathing pores'.

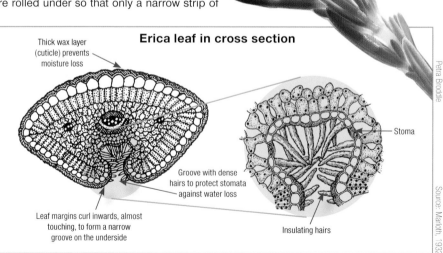

Thick wax layer (cuticle) prevents moisture loss

Erica leaf in cross section

Stoma

Groove with dense hairs to protect stomata against water loss

Leaf margins curl inwards, almost touching, to form a narrow groove on the underside

Insulating hairs

Petra Broddle

Source: Marloth, 1932

Most erica leaves are narrow and needle-like, with the margins rolled under to expose just a narrow groove on the leaf undersurface. This groove contains the breathing pores or stomata.

the underside is exposed along the midline. The 'breathing pores' or *stomata* of the leaves are confined to this narrow strip or groove, where dense hairs in the groove further insulate them from water loss. Shrinkage of the leaves during dry periods causes the edges of the blades to close even more tightly over the groove, sealing the pores off from the drying atmosphere. This protective mechanism against water loss enables ericas to survive the dry, windy Cape summers, even in the most exposed rocky situations.

Shuttering the stomata not only reduces water loss but also slows the uptake of gases from the atmosphere, such as the carbon dioxide necessary for photosynthesis. Ecologists measured the rate of photosynthesis in erica plants in Bain's Kloof above Wellington over the course of a year and

Nicky van Berkel

The edges of erica leaves are rolled under, helping to prevent water loss.

found that it was dramatically lower during the summer months. These periodic slowdowns in metabolic rates when they are under water stress ensure that erica plants make efficient use of the available water resources.

A REWARDING PARTNERSHIP

John Manning

Ericas growing in nutrient-poor soils obtain valuable nutrients from fungi that grow in assocation with their roots.

The roots of ericas are adapted to facilitate an intimate ecological partnership, or symbiosis, with certain types of soil fungi that allow them to thrive on the nutrient-poor soils that are characteristic of the Cape Floristic Region. These fungi or *mycorrhizae* take the place of the root hairs that develop near the tips of the roots in most other plants, and they are more effective than root hairs in their ability to extract scarce nutrients from the soil. The fungi transfer the nutrients to the erica roots in exchange for energy-rich carbohydrates produced by the plants through photosynthesis. These specially adapted roots are known as ericoid roots. We now know that several unrelated types of fungi are involved in this association.

POLLINATION OF ERICAS

Probably the most remarkable thing about Cape ericas, quite apart from the large number of species, is the diversity that they display in the shape, size and colour of their flowers. This variety appears to be directly linked to the preferred pollinators of each species but, as pollination has been studied in only some 20 *Erica* species, much remains to be discovered.

The great majority of ericas, probably some 80%, are thought to be pollinated by bees and other short-tongued insects, including day-flying burnet moths and flies. These insects visit most of the smaller-flowered species in the fynbos and around the world. The flowers of some of the insect-pollinated ericas are honey-scented. Unlike ericas elsewhere, however, Cape ericas have exploited several additional groups of pollinators.

The most important of these other pollinator groups are sunbirds, which probably pollinate well over 70 species, or 10%, of Cape ericas. These long-beaked, nectar-feeding birds typically visit and pollinate species of *Erica* with large, often brightly coloured, tubular flowers. The flowers of bird-pollinated ericas are often far more variable in colour than insect-pollinated species but why this should be so is not fully understood.

Most large-flowered Cape ericas, including *Erica coccinea*, are pollinated by sunbirds.

An Orange-breasted Sunbird sips nectar from an *Erica mammosa* flower.

A chafer beetle feeds on a profusion of white *Erica leucanthera* flowers.

The Cape Spiny Mouse is the main pollinator of two *Erica* species.

Long-proboscid horseflies and tangle-veined flies are another important, and very unusual, group of pollinators of an estimated 5% of Cape ericas. The adults of these large flies have long, syringe-like mouthparts that are adapted to sucking nectar. They visit ericas with medium-sized to large, slender or vase-shaped flowers with a narrow mouth and flaring petals, mostly coloured pale pink or white and often with a red eye around the mouth.

Recent studies suggest that moths may be the dominant pollinators of a few Cape ericas that produce pale, tubular flowers with a sweet or honeysuckle-like scent. Species with smaller, urn-shaped flowers like *Erica denticulata* are pollinated by settling moths but slender-tubed *Erica cylindrica* is one of relatively few plants in the Cape Floristic Region (CFR) that are pollinated by large, hovering hawkmoths. *Erica leucanthera*, which produces masses of creamy white or pale yellow, cup-shaped flowers, is regularly visited by flower chafer and monkey beetles and may be pollinated mainly by them.

Possibly some of the most intriguing pollinators of Cape ericas are rodents. Mice and gerbils are known to pollinate several Cape proteas and bulbs but the Cape Spiny Mouse has only recently been identified as the main pollinator of two ericas, *Erica hanekomii* from

A burnet moth probes the flowers of *Erica scytophylla* for nectar.

A horsefly pollinates *Erica irbyana* while extracting nectar with its long proboscis.

The flowers of *Erica verecunda* are a source of food for hoverflies.

This tangle-veined fly is a key pollinator of *Erica glandulifera*.

PYRAMIDS OF POLLEN GRAINS

Nick Helme

Courtesy of Saúl Manzano

Erica coccinea L. NBG278111

10 µm

Erica coccinea, like most ericas with 8 anthers, sheds its pollen in pyramidal stacks of 4 grains called pollen tetrads. These species also produce numerous ovules, and thus seeds, in each flower. By contrast, two-thirds of the smaller-flowered species with 4 anthers shed their pollen as solitary grains. These species mostly have just one or two ovules in each flower. Different ericas thus match the amount and packaging of their pollen to the number of ovules in their flowers. The 10µm scale bar = 0.01mm.

the Cederberg and *Erica lanuginosa* from the Kleinrivier Mountains. A few other species, including *Erica involucrata*, are certainly rodent-pollinated as well.

Finally, a significant number of ericas, comprising the remaining 5% of Cape species, rely on wind for their pollination. These species have small, inconspicuous flowers, often with well-exposed anthers, and widened, saucer-shaped stigmas that catch the wind-borne pollen grains. They typically lack the nectar glands at the base of the ovary that are found in the animal-pollinated species.

Ericas are unusual among flowering plants in that the great majority of species shed their pollen in parcels of 4 grains known as *pollen tetrads* rather than as solitary grains. Erica pollen tetrads are easily identifiable, and can be useful in crime scene investigations and in the identification and labelling of erica honey. They are also well preserved and easily identified in soil cores, and have proven useful in reconstructing past climate changes.

WHERE DO ERICAS OCCUR?

Ericas are widespread through the temperate parts of Africa, Europe and the Middle East, but the great majority of them are indigenous to South Africa. Some ericas have also been introduced to North America and a number are cultivated as ornamentals.

A total of some 860 species of ericas are recognised worldwide. Most of them, about 760 species, occur in southern Africa, and more particularly in the CFR, which is home to about 680 species, representing 80% of ericas worldwide. Nearly all of the Cape ericas are endemic (restricted) to the CFR, which extends from near Nieuwoudtville in the north to the Cape Peninsula in the south and eastwards along the coast and adjacent interior to Gqeberha (previously Port Elizabeth).

Source: Freiberg & Manning, 2013

Ericas are unevenly distributed through the CFR. A few species are widely distributed across the region but most are more restricted in their occurrence, sometimes to a single mountain range. The southwestern mountains are especially rich in *Erica* species.

Erica lucida (pink) and *Erica imbricata* (white), found in the Groot Winterhoek Mountains, are two of hundreds of *Erica* species that grow in the mountains of the Cape Floristic Region.

Ericas are found throughout the CFR but are most commonly associated with fynbos plant communities on sandstone, limestone and granite substrates. With a few notable exceptions, they are largely absent from the renosterveld shrublands found on clay soils.

Ericas are most diverse in well-watered mountainous areas, with some 300 different species or a little under half of the total in the region concentrated in the Kogelberg–Hottentots Holland mountain chain and adjacent mountains. This area is justly known as the heart of the CFR. High numbers of *Erica* species are also found on the mountains above Tulbagh and Ceres, and on the Cape Peninsula, where 100 or so different ericas occur. Relatively fewer species are found further north in the Cederberg or east on the Langeberg and Outeniqua–Tsitsikamma Mountains.

The very rare *Erica jasminiflora* grows in renosterveld shrubland.

Erica coccinea thrives on Constantiaberg on the Cape Peninsula.

WHERE DO ERICAS COME FROM?

The large number of species in the CFR is matched by the unique diversity of their flowers. This sets them apart from their tropical African and European relations, which have relatively undistinguished, small, bell-shaped flowers in shades of pink to purple. Plant geographers have long puzzled over the origin and evolutionary history of the plants in the CFR.

It is only very recently, through the application of powerful DNA-based techniques, that this question has been settled with some certainty. It is now clear that all of Africa's ericas represent a single evolutionary lineage derived from ancestral European stock, possibly as recently as 15 million years ago, and that the massive diversification of ericas in the CFR took place significantly more recently than this. These findings highlight the special place that Cape ericas occupy in our flora.

Corinne Merry

Extinct in the wild, *Erica verticillata* has been planted out in conservation areas.

ARE ERICAS RARE?

There are several aspects to rarity. A species could be considered to be naturally rare if it occurs only in a single very restricted area or in a specialised habitat, even if it is locally common where it occurs; or it may occur widely but only as scattered or occasional individuals. Rarity may be a reflection of past (and ongoing) threats to the continued survival of a species, and a species that was common and widespread in the past may since have lost some or even most of its populations.

The International Union for Conservation of Nature (IUCN) has developed a list of categories and criteria for assessing the conservation status of species as a means of highlighting those in need of conservation action (see box below). Those that have been assessed are placed on the IUCN Red List.

Nationally, one in four of South Africa's plant species faces some level of threat to its continued survival, but that number rises to one out of every three species in the CFR. These threats are especially acute in the lowlands, where most natural habitats have been lost to agriculture and urbanisation.

Ericas rank among the top 20 most threatened larger families of flowering plants in South Africa. Over 180 of South Africa's ericas, representing almost 20% of the species in the country, are Red Listed, indicating that they face some degree of threat to their survival, and at least one species, *Erica verticillata*, is extinct in the wild.

We include the conservation status for those species that fall into one of the categories of conservation concern.

SOUTH AFRICAN RED LIST CATEGORIES

EXTINCT no reasonable doubt that the last individual has died
CRITICALLY ENDANGERED facing an extremely high risk of extinction
ENDANGERED facing a very high risk of extinction
VULNERABLE facing a high risk of extinction
NEAR THREATENED likely to qualify for one of the above in the near future
CRITICALLY RARE occurring at only one site but not directly threatened
RARE rare but not directly threatened

IDENTIFYING ERICAS

The characters that are listed and briefly described below will introduce you to the exciting minutiae that constitute the world of the erica specialist, and will help you to accurately identify many of the species in this guide.

NOTES

Most of the characters critical for identifying ericas are very small, and a 10× hand-lens is essential for reliable identification. Naturally occurring hybrids have been recorded between quite a number of species in the wild. The hybrids usually occur as occasional or scattered individuals in mixed populations where the two parent species grow together, and do not appear to establish themselves more widely. Several of these hybrid individuals have been described as distinct species in the past. Bear this in mind as a possible source of confusion.

1 LEAVES The leaves of ericas are arranged in whorls of mostly 3 or 4, sometimes up to 6. The number of leaves in each whorl is often constant for each species and may be important in distinguishing between otherwise similar species, but is variable in others. The leaves are typically small, usually less than 10mm long, narrow and almost needle-like but sometimes broader and elliptical in shape. The leaves can be either hairless or hairy, often only along the margins. In addition, many species have stalkless glands or gland-tipped hairs along the leaf margins. The glandular tips of the hairs are not renewed once they have been abraded.

Nick Helme

The needle-like leaves of *Erica discolor* are arranged in whorls of 3 on the stems and short-shoots.

Ross Turner

The scale-like leaves of *Erica pectinifolia* are pressed against the stems in whorls of 4.

Nick Helme

The bristly leaves of *Erica cerinthoides* are arranged in whorls of 6.

❷ INFLORESCENCE The inflorescence is the arrangement of the flowers on the stems. Most ericas have small clusters of a few, often 3 or 4, flowers arising at the tips of the stems or branches. The flowering branches may be very short and contracted into specialised shoots termed short-shoots or spur-shoots, which arise in the axils of some of the leaves so that the flower clusters themselves appear to be axillary. These spur-shoots are often developed in a few axils near the top of the stems so that the individual inflorescences are aggregated into clusters, either whorls or false-spikes. In some species these spur-shoots are vestigial and represented by small stubs bearing a few minute scales, so that the flowers, which are usually solitary in such cases, arise directly in the upper leaf axils, forming racemes or heads.

The flowers of *Erica vestita* are arranged in a short, brush-like raceme near the ends of the stems.

group of 3 flowers

group of 4 flowers

In *Erica bergiana*, the globe-shaped flowers grow in groups of 3 or 4 at the tips of short-shoots.

short-shoot

The flowers of *Erica pectinifolia* appear at the tips of short-shoots and are more or less stalkless.

❸ FLOWER STALKS AND BRACTEOLES

Individual flowers are borne on a stalk or pedicel. This can be quite long but in some species is suppressed so that the flowers appear to be stalkless or sessile. Each flower stalk bears a small leaf-like bract near the base plus a pair of smaller bracteoles somewhere along its length, usually some distance below the tip, but in a few instances right at the top of the stalk, directly beneath the flower. The bracteoles are often scale-like or needle-like. In some species, however, they are larger and colourful, and may be difficult to distinguish from the sepals in those species in which they are pressed tightly up against the base of the calyx (ring of sepals). In a few species the bract and bracteoles have completely coalesced with the calyx during floral development, and such species thus have no discernible bracts or bracteoles.

The flower stalks of *Erica lateralis* can be short or slender.

In *Erica ampullacea* the stalks are suppressed and the bracteoles enlarged.

The bracteoles of *Erica regia* subsp. *regia* are needle-like.

In *Erica monsoniana*, the bracteoles are almost indistinguishable from the sepals.

❹ SEPALS The lowest whorl of each flower is made up of 4 sepals joined at the base to form a single whorl or calyx. In a few species the sepals are joined for half or more of their length in a cup-shaped or almost tubular calyx. In many species the individual sepals are small and lance-shaped or needle-like, but in some species they are larger, colourful and petal-like.

The sepals of *Erica albens* are leaf-shaped and papery.

Large, colourful and petal-like sepals characterise *Erica blenna*.

In *Erica plukenetii* subsp. *plukenetii*, the sepals are lance-shaped and colourful.

The large, petal-like sepals of *Erica thunbergii* are papery and loose.

❺ COROLLA Above the calyx are the petals, generally forming the most conspicuous part of the flower. The petals of all ericas are joined for most of their length to form a more or less cylindrical corolla (ring of petals) that is 4-lobed at the tip. The lobes are usually short and rounded or blunt, but in some species are more sharply pointed. The shape and length of the tubular portion of the corolla is often diagnostic.

The surface of the corolla in fresh flowers is either hairless or covered in short, velvety hairs. In most species the corolla is more or less dry but in others, especially those with larger flowers, it is coated with a sticky or tacky covering as if freshly varnished. The sticky varnish in these species comes from glands on the inner surface of the sepals that secrete a biological varnish onto the outside of the corolla while it is still enclosed by the sepals in bud.

Flower colour can be very variable in a single species, especially among the larger-flowered ericas. Different populations in some of these species may have differently coloured flowers, either plain or banded in a combination of different hues. This is less common among the smaller-flowered species, many of which are consistently whitish or pink to purple.

Globe-shaped: The corolla of *Erica multumbellifera* is almost spherical but abruptly narrows to a small mouth.

Urn-shaped: In *Erica sphaerocephala* the corolla is swollen at the base and narrows evenly towards the mouth.

Vase-shaped: In both *Erica lutea* (above left) and *Erica junonia* (above right), the corolla is swollen at the base and then narrows into a distinct short or long neck.

A COAT OF VARNISH

The Cape Town botanist Louisa Bolus (1877–1970) proposed in the 1920s that the sticky exudate that coats the outside of the corolla of several of the larger-flowered ericas, '*besides keeping crawlers* [crawling insects] *away from the nectar supply, might help make the flowers last fresh for much longer than is usual in heaths*'. It is only recently that scientists have confirmed both of these suggested benefits of the sticky varnish: as a sealant preventing the flowers from drying out and as a form of biological flypaper discouraging non-pollinating insects from robbing the flowers of their nectar. The sticky varnish is most prevalent among the larger-flowered ericas.

John Manning

John Manning

Cup-shaped: *Erica paniculata* has the corolla hemispherical with the mouth wide and the lobes relatively small, erect or slightly spreading.

Ross Turner

Tubular: In *Erica cylindrica* the corolla is more or less cylindrical throughout.

Goblet-shaped: The hemispherical corolla of *Erica cubica* narrows below the mouth and then widens, with the large, cupped lobes as long as or longer than the tube.

⑥ STAMENS AND ANTHERS

Most species have 8 stamens, although a number of them have just 4. Each stamen is made up of a long, thread-like stalk or filament that carries an anther at its tip. In many species the anthers are enclosed or included within the corolla tube, but in others they protrude well beyond the mouth of the corolla tube and are thus very visible. Each anther comprises 2 small sacs containing the pollen grains. The pollen grains of ericas are dry and dust-like, and they are readily shaken out of the anthers through a short pore that opens near the tip of each sac. The anther sacs are either closely pressed together along their inner edges or are separated for some or much of their length so that the anthers are distinctly forked or V-shaped. Curiously, the anthers of ericas and other members of the Ericaceae are tipped upwards during their early development so that the real bottom is uppermost in the mature anther.

The anthers are dark brown or almost black in colour, with the singular exception of *Erica leucanthera*, which has pale yellow anthers. The base of each sac where it attaches to the filament often bears a small horn-like spur or toothed crest, often brown or reddish but pure white in some species. The shape and size of the anthers' appendages are important for distinguishing different species.

The flowers of *Erica ericoides* have 4 stamens.

Erica scytophylla has 8 stamens.

The anthers of *Erica gysbertii* are concealed in the corolla tube.

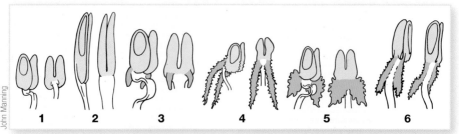

Erica species differ in the size and shape of their anthers and the type of appendages at the base: **1.** Short anthers, rounded at the base; **2.** Long anthers, tapering at the base; **3.** Smooth spurs or short horns at the base; **4.** Long, hairy or bristly tails at the base; **5.** Toothed crests at the base; **6.** Long hairy tails that are partially joined at their base to the filament.

❼ STIGMA The ovary in the base of the flower is topped with a thread-like style that ends in a stigma. In most species the stigma is slightly swollen and pinhead-like, but in some of the smaller-flowered species it is conspicuously widened and saucer- or disc-shaped.

Stigmas are disc- or saucer-shaped in *Erica hispidula* (top) and in *Erica coarctata* (above).

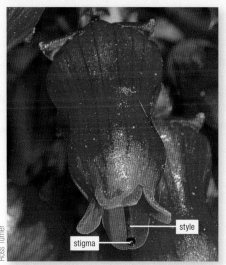

In most species, such as *Erica inordinata*, the stigma is in the shape of a pinhead.

❽ OVARY AND FRUIT The ovary ripens into the fruit. Most species have the ovary divided internally into 4 wedge-shaped chambers, but a few species have 6 or 8 chambers in each ovary, each chamber containing many ovules that develop into the seeds. In all of these species the mature fruit has thick, woody walls that split open, or dehisce, from the top into sections, allowing the numerous small seeds contained in each chamber to be shed. In contrast to this, a group of smaller-flowered species have 1- or 2-chambered ovaries with just 1 or 2 ovules in each chamber. In these species the ovary matures into a fruit with a thin, papery or membranous wall that does not split open but gradually decays to release the seeds long after the fruit has been shed onto the ground.

The ovary and stamens of *Erica albens*

❾ DISTRIBUTION Many ericas are more or less restricted in their distribution, often to a few adjacent mountain ranges. One of the clearest breaks is that between species that occur on the mountains west of Bredasdorp–Riviersonderend and those from the southern coastal ranges east of Bredasdorp. Check the distribution data carefully before making an identification.

Ring out so clear, so sweet –
Silver Heath of Riversdale

John Runcie,
'The Bells of Allah'

Erica pillansii
in bloom
(foreground)
Colin Paterson-Jones

ABOUT THIS BOOK

This guide features 180 species, or just over a quarter, of the 680 species of *Erica* found in the CFR. The species were selected primarily from among the 200 ericas with the highest number of sightings logged on the iNaturalist online identification platform (www.inaturalist. org). From this list we chose species with larger and more colourful flowers, followed by the most common of the smaller-flowered species. We also included a small selection of very distinctive or unusual species, some of them very rare or localised in their distribution but likely to attract attention when seen. We have included only a few species of the so-called minor genera, as they are impossible to tell apart without using a microscope.

Quick guide to groups

Even when in bloom, telling *Erica* species apart can be extremely challenging. To aid identification, the species presented in this book have been divided into five groups based on similar diagnostic features. Within each group, they have been organised into smaller clusters. These are associations of convenience that do not necessarily indicate true evolutionary groupings.

Common names

A few Cape ericas have long-standing vernacular or common names but they are in the minority. For the rest we have mostly translated the botanical name into English as a convenient way of providing a more accessible name.

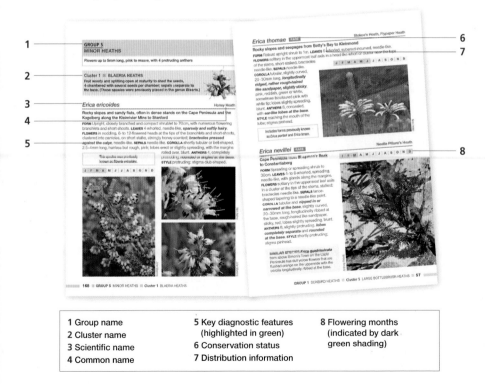

1 Group name	5 Key diagnostic features (highlighted in green)
2 Cluster name	6 Conservation status
3 Scientific name	7 Distribution information
4 Common name	8 Flowering months (indicated by dark green shading)

THE SPECIES

There is no clear idea yet on relationships among most *Erica* species. To assist in identifying Cape ericas we have divided the species into **GROUPS** based on a few obvious floral characters. Some of these groups are clearly linked to the pollination systems that are exploited by the species in those groups. Within the main groups we have also identified smaller **CLUSTERS** of species.

GROUP 1
SUNBIRD HEATHS

Flowers large, the corolla mostly more than 10mm long, tubular or urn-shaped and often slightly curved, with relatively small rounded lobes erect or flaring around the mouth

urn-shaped corolla

small rounded lobe, ±erect at the mouth

Erica monsoniana

small rounded lobe, ±flaring at the mouth

long, curving tubular corolla

Erica perspicua

GROUP 2
VASE HEATHS

Flowers with a straight, vase-shaped or very narrowly tubular corolla, with a small, pinhole mouth and recurved or spreading star-like lobes, often pink with a dark throat or ring around the mouth

spreading star-like lobes

straight, narrowly vase-shaped corolla

Erica junonia

vase-shaped corolla

small pinhole mouth

Erica retorta

GROUP 3
SMALL-FLOWER HEATHS

Smaller-flowered species with an urn- or goblet-shaped corolla 3–10mm long with 8 anthers

Erica thunbergii

Erica parilis

GROUP 4
STOPPERED HEATHS

Flowers minute, cup-shaped, 1–1.5mm long, with 8 anthers and the mouth of the corolla ±blocked or covered by a large saucer-shaped stigma

Erica hispidula

GROUP 5
MINOR HEATHS

Flowers up to 5mm long, pink to mauve, with 4 protruding anthers

Erica uberiflora

GROUP 1
SUNBIRD HEATHS

Flowers large, the corolla mostly more than 10mm long, tubular or urn-shaped and often slightly curved, with relatively small rounded lobes erect or flaring around the mouth

Cluster 1 ■ TASSEL HEATHS
Anthers long and stick-like, protruding well beyond the mouth of the corolla

Erica plukenetii   Brown-tongue Heath, Plukenet's Heath, Hangertjie, Spagettiheide

Namaqualand and throughout the southwestern mountains from near Nieuwoudtville to Mossel Bay and inland on the Witteberg

FORM Upright bushy shrublet 30–100cm. **LEAVES** 3-whorled and in axillary tufts or short-shoots, erect and curved inwards, needle-like, hairless or hairy. **FLOWERS** mostly solitary on the axillary short-shoots arranged in false-spikes towards the ends of the main branches, pendulous on nodding stalks; *bracteoles scale-like, near the base of the flower stalks*. **SEPALS** lance-shaped or almost petal-like, reddish or green. **COROLLA** tubular or urn-shaped, (7–)10–18mm long, hairless, reddish or whitish with darker tips; lobes erect and small. **ANTHERS** 8, protruding, long and stick-like, tapering at the base. **STYLE** protruding; stigma pinhead.

The longer-flowered forms are pollinated by sunbirds but subsp. *breviflora* with short, white flowers is pollinated primarily by settling moths.

| J | F | M | A | M | J | J | A | S | O | N | D |

FIVE SUBSPECIES This is a variable species with four subspecies differing mainly in the size and shape of their sepals and the fifth in the size of its flowers: subsp. *plukenetii* is widespread and has variably lance-shaped to oval sepals 2–7mm long; subsp. *bredensis* and subsp. *lineata* from limestone hills and coastal flats between Gansbaai and Cape Infanta have very broad, elliptical, petal-like sepals 5–6mm long that overlap for most of their length in two opposite pairs; subsp. *penicellata* from the Kleinrivier and Riviersonderend Mtns to Bredasdorp has long, lance-shaped sepals up to 12mm long that are 2-keeled with a very broad median groove; and subsp. *breviflora* from the Cederberg to the Franschhoek Mtns is distinctive in its short, white or rarely pink flowers 7–12mm long.

Ross Turner

subsp. *plukenetii*

subsp. *plukenetii*

subsp. *breviflora*

subsp. *lineata*

subsp. *penicellata*

Erica coccinea

Tassel Heath, Hangertjie

Throughout the southwestern mountains and on rocky flats from the Cederberg to the Cape Peninsula and eastwards through the Langeberg and Outeniqua Mtns to George

FORM Upright bushy shrublet with stems to 1m, closely covered with short-shoots, sometimes coppicing from the rootstock. **LEAVES** densely 3-whorled on short-shoots, *often spreading or curved outwards*, needle-like. **FLOWERS** mostly in 3s at the tips of the short-shoots arranged in dense false-spikes towards the ends of the main branches, pendulous on nodding stalks; *bracteoles sepal-like, clasping the calyx.* **SEPALS** lance-shaped or almost petal-like, coloured like the corolla, with glands along the margins. **COROLLA** tubular or urn-shaped, 10–18mm long, hairless (or rarely hairy), often slightly sticky, red or yellow to greenish; lobes erect and small. **ANTHERS** 8, protruding, long and stick-like, tapering at the base. **STYLE** protruding; stigma pinhead.

J	F	M	A	M	J	J	A	S	O	N	D

TWO SUBSPECIES subsp. *coccinea* has flowers in 3s at the tips of the short-shoots; and subsp. *uniflora* from coastal lowlands between Simon's Town and Mossel Bay has a solitary flower on each short-shoot.

subsp. *uniflora*

subsp. *coccinea*

subsp. *coccinea*

Erica intermedia

Southern coastal mountains on the Langeberg and Outeniqua Mtns from Swellendam to George

This species is very like a smaller-flowered form of **Erica coccinea** with a green to yellowish green or white corolla 6–11mm long, but the **tips of the anthers are sharp** and **almost prickle-like** rather than blunt as in the other species in this group.

J	F	M	A	M	J	J	A	S	O	N	D

TWO SUBSPECIES subsp. **intermedia** has a green to yellow-green corolla 8–11mm long; and smaller-flowered subsp. **albiflora** from around the Robinson Pass in the Outeniqua Mtns has a white corolla 6mm long.

subsp. *intermedia*

Rendert Hoekstra

Erica melastoma

Black-mouthed Tassel Heath

Throughout the southwestern mountains from the Cederberg to the Hottentots Holland Mtns to Agulhas

FORM Upright bushy shrublet with stems to 1m, closely covered with short-shoots. **LEAVES** densely 3-whorled on short-shoots, needle-like, **suberect and straight** (not spreading or curved outwards), with minute forward-pointing bristles or barbs along the margins. **FLOWERS** solitary at the tips of the short-shoots arranged in dense false-spikes towards the ends of the main branches, pendulous on nodding stalks; bracteoles sepal-like, clasping the calyx. **SEPALS** lance-shaped or almost petal-like, **not grooved down the centre**, coloured like the corolla, with glands along the margins. **COROLLA** urn-shaped, usually 18mm long but 6–7mm long in subsp. **minor**, hairless, slightly sticky, greenish yellow, or yellow-orange, and often with a brownish tip; lobes erect, **narrow**, sometimes more than half as long as the corolla tube. **ANTHERS** 8, protruding, long and stick-like, tapering at the base. **STYLE** protruding; stigma pinhead.

Rather similar to *Erica coccinea* (see p. 34) but with straight leaves, sepals without a groove down the centre, and longer, more pointed corolla lobes.

J	F	M	A	M	J	J	A	S	O	N	D

TWO SUBSPECIES Larger-flowered subsp. **melastoma** has a corolla 18mm long and rather variable in shape, colour and stickiness; and smaller-flowered subsp. **minor** from the mountains between Hermanus and Bredasdorp has a corolla 6–7mm long and always yellow with a dark mouth.

subsp. *melastoma*

subsp. *melastoma*

subsp. *melastoma*

Nick Helme

Ross Turner

Ross Turner

Erica monadelphia
False Tassel Heath

Cape Peninsula from Muizenberg to
Cape Point, and from Betty's Bay
to Potberg

FORM Upright bushy shrublet with stems to
90cm, closely covered with short-shoots.
LEAVES densely 3-whorled on short-shoots,
needle-like. **FLOWERS** mostly in 3s at the tips
of the short-shoots, arranged in false-spikes
towards the ends of the main branches,
pendulous on nodding stalks; *bracteoles
sepal-like, clasping the calyx*. **SEPALS** petal-
like, red or yellow. **COROLLA** tubular, 10–
13mm long, hairless, sticky, red; lobes
erect and small. **ANTHERS** 8, protruding,
tapering at the base, on thick protruding
*filaments that are kinked below the
anthers*. **STYLE** protruding; stigma pinhead.

Corinne Merry

| J | F | M | A | M | J | J | A | S | O | N | D |

Erica banksii
Banks's Heath, Green Tutu Heath

Hottentots Holland Mtns to near Bredasdorp

This species was formerly
incorrectly spelled *Erica banksia*.

FORM Sprawling rounded shrublet. **LEAVES** 3-whorled,
needle-like. **FLOWERS** in 3s at the branch tips,
pendulous, almost stalkless; *bracteoles
sepal-like, clasping the calyx*, hairless.
SEPALS greenish or pink, with *needle-like tips*.
COROLLA tubular, 14–20mm long, hairless,
whitish, yellow or pink, with contrasting
red tip; *lobes spreading and pointed*.
ANTHERS 8, protruding, tapering at the
base, on thick protruding *filaments* that are
kinked below the anthers. **STYLE** protruding;
stigma pinhead.

John Manning

subsp. *banksii*

| J | F | M | A | M | J | J | A | S | O | N | D |

THREE SUBSPECIES subsp. *banksii* from
around Elgin in the Hottentots Holland Mtns
has short leaves 5–6mm long and pale green
flowers with darker lobes; subsp. *comptonii*
(= *Erica comptonii*) from the Kogelberg,
also with pale green flowers, has longer,
awn-tipped leaves 12–26mm long; and
subsp. *purpurea* from the Kleinrivier Mtns has
distinctive flowers with a white corolla tube
and purple lobes, and leaves 5–9mm long.

Ross Turner

subsp. *purpurea*

Erica monsoniana

Lady Monson's Heath, Large White Papery Heath,
Snow Heath, Sneeuheide

Cederberg southwards to the Hottentots Holland Mtns and thence east to Potberg

FORM Upright shrub with rod-like stems 1.2–1.8m, with numerous ascending flowering short-shoots arising successively up the stems, forming conifer-like plumes; the young stems are densely felted with plumed hairs. **LEAVES** 3-whorled, needle-like; the uppermost leaves immediately below the flowers are broadened, with papery margins and resemble the bracts. **FLOWERS** 1 to 3 at the tips of the short-shoots, aggregated in a dense false-raceme towards the end of the stem, like an alabaster column, nodding on short stalks; *bracteoles pressed against the calyx*, broad and papery, petal-like and coloured like the corolla. **SEPALS** large, papery and petal-like, elliptical with a keeled tip, ±half as long as the corolla and coloured like it. **COROLLA** urn-shaped, *15–20mm long*, hairless, chalk-white; lobes erect, pointed. **ANTHERS** 8, concealed, with crests at the base that are partially joined to the filaments. **STYLE** concealed; stigma pinhead.

J F M A M J J A S O N D

John Manning

Nick Helme

Erica glauca

Cup-and-saucer Heath, Kommetjie-pieringheide

Along the western mountains from the Koue Bokkeveld north of Ceres and the
Hex River Mtns to Wellington and Franschhoek

FORM Upright or willowy shrublet or shrub to 1.8m, with sparse flowering short-shoots
towards the ends of the stems; the stems are smooth and hairless. **LEAVES** 3-whorled, needle-
like, *smooth and hairless with a grey bloom*; the uppermost leaves immediately below
the flowers are broadened, with papery margins and resemble the bracts. **FLOWERS** 4 to 7
at the tips of the branches and short-shoots, nodding on stalks; *bracteoles arising well
below the sepals*, broad and papery, petal-like and coloured like the sepals. **SEPALS** large,
papery and petal-like, elliptical with a keeled tip, ±half as long as the corolla and spreading

or ±as long as the corolla and enclosing it,
either red with the corolla dull reddish and
purple *or* pale pink with the corolla pale
greenish white. **COROLLA** sac-like with a
swollen base narrowed to a relatively long
neck, 8–12mm long, hairless, leathery,
either greenish white or dull red with a
purple neck and mouth; lobes small, curved
outward, pointed. **ANTHERS** 8, concealed,
with large crests at the base that are
sometimes partially joined to the filaments.
STYLE concealed; stigma pinhead.

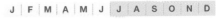

J | F | M | A | M | J | J | A | S | O | N | D

Nick Helme

Nick Helme

Erica blenna Lantern Heath, Orange-and-green Heath, Belletjiesheide

Moist southern slopes of the Langeberg Mtns from Swellendam to Riversdale

FORM Upright, sparsely branched shrublet to 1.5m, with wand-like or willowy stems bearing scattered branchlets or short-shoots. **LEAVES** 3-whorled, needle-like, minutely toothed with scattered glands along the margins. **FLOWERS** 1 to 3 at the tips of a few short-shoots towards the ends of the stems, occasionally aggregated in a whorl, nodding on long stalks; bracteoles lance-shaped with glands along the margins. **SEPALS** large and lance-shaped or petal-like, rather loose, with the margins rolled in, sticky, yellowish or orange. **COROLLA** urn-shaped and almost bladder-like, constricted at the top of the tube into a very small mouth, 10–20mm long, *hairless and very sticky, yellow or orange; lobes green*, erect, rounded. **ANTHERS** 8, concealed, with jagged crests at the base. **STYLE** concealed or just protruding from the mouth; stigma pinhead.

Ross Turner

Ross Turner

Nick Helme

Erica halicacaba RARE

Gooseberry Heath

Cape Peninsula

FORM Gnarled, woody shrub to 1m, often pressed against rocks, with numerous, densely leafy branchlets bearing short-shoots. **LEAVES** 3-whorled but very closely packed, suberect and curving outwards, needle-like, with minute prickle-like hairs along the margins when young. **FLOWERS** 1 to 3 at the tips of a few of the short-shoots towards the ends of the branches, nodding on short stalks; *bracteoles ±pressed against the calyx*, lance-shaped and papery, petal-like and coloured like the corolla. **SEPALS** large, papery and petal-like, broad below and overlapping in two opposite pairs, tapered and pointed, less than half as long as the corolla and coloured like it. **COROLLA** egg-shaped with the *mouth closed by the lobes*, 16–20mm long, *hairless, pale celadon-green; lobes erect and furled like an umbrella, forming a spout, pointed*. **ANTHERS** 8, concealed, with minute awns at the base that are partially joined to the filaments. **STYLE** concealed; stigma pinhead.

J | F | M | A | M | J | J | A | S | O | N | D

The unusual gooseberry-like flowers are pollinated by Orange-breasted Sunbirds.

Ross Turner

John Manning

Nick Helme

Cluster 3 ■ SEPALINE HEATHS
Sepals more prominent than the corolla and mostly or fully concealing it

Erica lanuginosa
Downy Heath

Kleinrivier Mtns from Hermanus to Stanford

FORM Upright or spreading, mat-forming woody shrublet to 60cm, with distinctive flowers resembling Cape Gooseberries almost hidden among the long leaves. **LEAVES** 3-whorled, often arching inwards but the lower leaves sometimes spreading or curved back, needle-like, mostly 15–20mm long, fringed with silky hairs along the margins when young. **FLOWERS** solitary or in 3s on reduced short-shoots in the upper leaf axils, often forming loose clusters towards the branch tips, nodding on short, stout, densely velvety or felted stalks; bracteoles leaf-shaped, loosely pressed against the calyx, velvety and fringed with shaggy hairs along the margins. **SEPALS** *large and leaf-shaped, concealing the lower two-thirds of the corolla, velvety and fringed with shaggy hairs* along the margins, dull reddish brown. **COROLLA** egg-shaped, *divided almost to the base with an almost obsolete tube* bearing an additional small, flap-like tooth hidden between the lobes, 14–18mm long, *hairless below but velvety above* with densely felted tips, white; *lobes long and tapering, stiffly erect and forming a stout beak, pointed*. **ANTHERS** concealed within the beak, with long horns at the base. **STYLE** concealed within the beak; stigma pinhead.

J | F | M | A | M | J | J | A | S | O | N | D

Mo Oliver

Erica nabea

Moist flats and slopes on the Outeniqua, Tsitsikamma and Kouga Mtns from George to Kariega

FORM Upright, wand-like shrublet to 1.5m, the stems closely covered with leafy short-shoots. **LEAVES** 3-whorled, needle-like, conspicuously fringed with hairs along the margins, the primary leaves mostly 10–15mm long but soon falling and developing a short-shoot in the axil so that the stems resemble leafy bottlebrushes. **FLOWERS** 1 or 2 at the tips of the upper short-shoots, forming short or long false-spikes, *erect, ±stalkless*; bracteoles lance-shaped and papery, ±half as long as the sepals. **SEPALS** *large* and *narrowly lance-shaped, closely pressed together in two opposite pairs* and *narrowed above to form a 'beak', 12–15mm* long, the outer pair lance-shaped and enclosing the inner pair, which are paddle-shaped at the tips, concealing the corolla and stamens, white with a green midrib. **COROLLA** *deeply hidden within the calyx, narrowly urn-shaped, 3–4mm* long, hairless, white; lobes erect, rounded. **ANTHERS** protruding well beyond the corolla on long filaments reaching nearly to the tips of the sepals but remaining hidden within them, rounded at the base. **STYLE** almost reaching the tips of the sepals but *hooked like a crook at the end*, and *remaining hidden*; stigma pinhead.

| J | F | M | A | M | J | J | A | S | O | N | D |

Ross Turner

Nicky van Berkel

Cluster 4 ■ CLUSTER HEATHS
Flowers in nodding heads at the branch tips,
usually ±stalkless, with a velvety or hairy corolla

Erica strigilifolia
Bristle-leaved Heath

Swartberg to the Kouga Mtns

J	F	M	A	M	J	J	A	S	O	N	D

FORM Rounded shrublet to 60cm.
LEAVES 4-whorled, elliptical, finely velvety
when young and *fringed on the margins*
with *short, velvety bristles, greyish*.
FLOWERS in nodding 4-flowered heads at
the tips of short side-shoots, ±stalkless;
bracteoles lance-shaped, velvety and
fringed with bristles. **SEPALS** lance-
shaped, velvety and *fringed with bristles*.
COROLLA tubular, 14–18mm long, finely
velvety and also with *shaggy, bristle-like
hairs in the upper half*, white or pink
to carmine-red; lobes erect, rounded.
ANTHERS 8, concealed, *rounded at the
base*. **STYLE** concealed; stigma pinhead.

Ross Turner

Nick Helme

Erica pectinifolia
Comb-leaved Heath

Uniondale to Gqeberha

FORM Willowy shrublet to 1.8m. **LEAVES** 4-whorled, needle-like, finely velvety when young and *fringed on the margins* with *short, velvety bristles*. **FLOWERS** in nodding 4-flowered heads at the tips of short side-shoots, ±stalkless; bracteoles lance-shaped, velvety and fringed with bristles. **SEPALS** lance-shaped with a *narrower, stalk-like base*, velvety and *fringed with bristles*. **COROLLA** club-shaped and slightly swollen in the upper part then narrowed to the mouth, 14–18mm long, finely velvety and also *with shaggy, bristle-like hairs in the upper half*, white to pale pink or bicoloured; lobes erect, rounded. **ANTHERS** 8, concealed, *spurred at the base*. **STYLE** shortly protruding; stigma pinhead.

J	F	M	A	M	J	J	A	S	O	N	D

John Manning

Ross Turner

Ross Turner

Erica sparrmanii

Sparrman's Heath

Uniondale to Humansdorp

FORM Willowy or lanky shrublet to 1.9m.
LEAVES 4-whorled, needle-like, *glossy* and
covered with glassy bristles. **FLOWERS** in
nodding 4-flowered heads at the tips of
short side-shoots, ±stalkless; bracteoles
lance-shaped, with yellow glassy bristles
in the upper half. **SEPALS** lance-shaped,
covered with yellow glassy bristles in the
upper half. **COROLLA** tubular and slightly
swollen at the tip, 12–18mm long, *densely*
covered with shaggy, yellow, bristle-like
hairs, yellow to lime-green; lobes erect
and almost closing the mouth, pointed.
ANTHERS 8, concealed, shortly spurred.
STYLE shortly protruding; stigma pinhead.

J	F	M	A	M	J	J	A	S	O	N	D

Ross Turner

Ross Turner

Erica tumida

Rocky sandstone slopes from the Cederberg to the Hex River Mtns

| J | F | M | A | M | J | J | A | S | O | N | D |

FORM Upright or spreading, rounded shrub to 1.5m, closely covered with short-shoots in the upper parts. **LEAVES** 4-whorled on stems, needle-like, *velvety, ashy-grey*. **FLOWERS** 1 to 4 at the tips of branchlets aggregated in dense clusters, long-stalked; bracteoles lance-shaped, velvety with gland-tipped bristles along the margins, often ±pressed against the calyx. **SEPALS** lance-shaped, *velvety* with *conspicuous, gland-tipped bristles towards the edges* and *along the margins*. **COROLLA** somewhat urn-shaped, curved, 12–25mm long, velvety, *dark pink to red*; lobes spreading, blunt. **ANTHERS** 8, concealed, with *jagged horns at the base*. **STYLE** reaching the mouth of the tube; stigma pinhead.

Nick Helme

Erica brachialis VULNERABLE

Coastal rocky slopes close to the seashore on the Cape Peninsula from Llandudno to Cape Point, and Rooi Els to Pringle Bay

FORM Sturdy shrub to 2m, with trunks up to 30mm in diameter; branchlets often spreading widely. **LEAVES** 4- to 6-whorled, closely overlapping, needle-like, *minutely saw-toothed* and *glandular along the margins*. **FLOWERS** mostly 2 to 6 at the tips of branchlets, stalked; bracteoles needle-like, sometimes pressed against the calyx. **SEPALS** lance-shaped.

| J | F | M | A | M | J | J | A | S | O | N | D |

COROLLA tubular but *becoming urn-shaped with a swollen base as the fruit matures*, 14–16mm long, velvety, pale green fading yellow; lobes erect or slightly spreading, blunt. **ANTHERS** 8, *deeply enclosed in the tube on kinked filaments*, spurred at the base. **STYLE** shortly protruding; stigma pinhead. **FRUIT** *conspicuous globular woody capsules 5mm* long that persist on the plants for some years.

Nick Helme

Erica cerinthoides

Fire Heath, Rooihaartjie

Widespread on mountain slopes and flats from the Cederberg to the Cape Peninsula eastwards through the Eastern Cape and along the Drakensberg to Mpumalanga

FORM Erect shrublet, *resprouting after fire*, at length willowy and up to 1.9m. **LEAVES** 4- to 6-whorled, needle-like, variably velvety or hairy with gland-tipped bristles or fringed with short bristles along the margins, erect or curved outwards. **FLOWERS** nodding in head-like clusters at the stem tips, stalked; bracteoles lance-shaped, *one or both pressed to the sepals, sticky with gland-tipped hairs.* **SEPALS** lance-shaped, *sticky with gland-tipped hairs or bristles.* **COROLLA** club-shaped or slightly swollen near the middle, 12–35mm long, *velvety* and *with sticky hairs, orange-red to pinkish red* (cream-coloured with red tips along the Drakensberg); lobes erect, rounded. **ANTHERS** 8, concealed, *rounded or minutely awned.* **STYLE** shortly protruding; stigma pinhead.

Plants flower especially well after fire.

J	F	M	A	M	J	J	A	S	O	N	D

Nick Helme

Cluster 5 ■ LARGE BOTTLEBRUSH HEATHS

Flowers solitary in the axils of the upper leaves, arranged in whorls or racemes towards the tops of the stems

Erica baueri ENDANGERED

Bridal Heath, Bauer's Heath

Sandy flats around Albertinia and Still Bay

FORM Upright shrub with lanky stems to 1.5m. **LEAVES** 4-whorled, needle-like, spreading or arching, *greyish*. **FLOWERS** solitary or paired in upper leaf axils in a cluster near the tips of the stems, stalked; bracteoles scale-like. **SEPALS** *leaf-shaped*. **COROLLA** narrowly urn-shaped, slightly curved, 15–20mm long, *velvety, white or pale to mauve-pink*; lobes spreading, blunt. **ANTHERS** 8, concealed, long-spurred at the base with a conspicuous chin. **STYLE** reaching the mouth of the tube; stigma pinhead.

This species was formerly incorrectly spelled *Erica bauera*.

J | F | M | A | M | J | J | A | S | O | N | D

TWO SUBSPECIES subsp. *baueri* has spreading leaves and spike-like clusters of 10 to 20 flowers; and subsp. *gouriquae* has erect leaves and shorter clusters of 5 to 20 flowers.

subsp. *baueri*

Sandra Falanga

subsp. *baueri*

John Manning

Erica penduliflora

Pendent-flower Heath

Sandy hills and flats from Pearly Beach to Viljoenshof

FORM Upright shrub with lanky stems to 1m. **LEAVES** 4-whorled, needle-like, erect. **FLOWERS** solitary or in upper leaf axils in a short raceme near the tips of the stems, stalked; bracteoles scale-like. **SEPALS** *broadly leaf-shaped*. **COROLLA** narrowly urn-shaped, 12–18mm long, *hairless, white or yellowish green*; lobes erect, blunt. **ANTHERS** 8, concealed, with long horn-like spurs at the base and a conspicuous chin. **STYLE** reaching the mouth of the tube; stigma pinhead.

| J | F | M | A | M | J | J | A | S | O | N | D |

Liz Hutton

John Manning

John Manning

Erica mammosa

Sandy flats and slopes from the Cederberg to the Cape Peninsula and east to Bredasdorp
FORM Upright shrub to 1.8m. **LEAVES** 4- to 6-whorled, needle-like. **FLOWERS** solitary or paired in the upper leaf axils in a short raceme near the tips of the stems, stalked; bracteoles scale-like. **SEPALS** lance-shaped and papery along the sides. **COROLLA** narrowly urn-shaped with *4 dents or furrows at the base*, slightly curved, 15–25mm long, hairless, red, orange, pink, green or white with pink tips; lobes spreading, blunt. **ANTHERS** 8, concealed, with a nose-like protuberance at the base and long-spurred. **STYLE** reaching the mouth of the tube; stigma pinhead.

Includes pale creamy-coloured plants that were formerly treated as *Erica gilva*.

| J | F | M | A | M | J | J | A | S | O | N | D |

Erica sessiliflora

Bottlebrush Heath, Green Trumpet Heath

Damp sandy flats and slopes from Piketberg and the Koue Bokkeveld to the Cape Peninsula and east through the southern coastal ranges to Humansdorp

FORM Upright shrub to 2m. **LEAVES** 4- to 6-whorled, spreading or incurved, needle-like with a slender sharp point. **FLOWERS** crowded in the uppermost leaf *axils in a head-like spike at the tips of the stems, stalkless*; the *fruiting spikes remaining for several years, like corncobs*; bracteoles lance-shaped. **SEPALS** lance-shaped, *hard but papery* along the sides, *sometimes coloured, enlarging* and becoming *uniquely fleshy in fruit*. **COROLLA** tubular, slightly curved, 15–25mm long, hairless, pale green; lobes erect, blunt. **ANTHERS** 8, concealed, with a nose-like protuberance at the base and long-spurred. **STYLE** reaching the mouth of the tube; stigma pinhead.

Erica abietina

Restricted to rocky slopes on the Cape Peninsula

FORM Upright shrub to 1.5m. **LEAVES** 4- to 6-whorled, needle-like, sometimes up to 20mm long, slightly sticky. **FLOWERS** solitary in the upper leaf axils in a head-like cluster near the tops of the stems, short-stalked; bracteoles needle-like. **SEPALS** lance-shaped, tapering to a needle-like point, glossy, hairless or minutely hairy, slightly sticky. **COROLLA** tubular, slightly curved, 8–26mm long, hairless or sparsely hairy, slightly sticky, red or pale to deep pink or purple; lobes slightly spreading, blunt. **ANTHERS** 8, concealed or well exserted, *lobes completely separate* and *rounded at the base*. **OVARY** covered with *velvety, down-pointing hairs*. **STYLE** shortly protruding; stigma pinhead.

This species includes forms previously known as *Erica conica* and *Erica phylicifolia*.

FOUR SUBSPECIES subsp. *abietina* from the upper slopes and plateau of Table Mountain has red flowers 18–26mm long; subsp. *atrorosea* (= *Erica phylicifolia*) from the lower slopes of Table Mountain south to Cape Point has rose-pink flowers 18–22mm long; subsp. *diabolis* from Devil's Peak saddle has shorter, rose-pink flowers 11–14mm long; and subsp. *constantiana* (= *Erica conica*) from Constantiaberg has short, rose-pink flowers 8–11mm long.

| J | F | M | A | M | J | J | A | S | O | N | D |

subsp. *abietina*

Nick Helme

John Manning

subsp. *abietina*

Corinne Merry

subsp. *constantiana*

Nick Helme

subsp. *atrorosea*

Erica grandiflora

Large-flowered Heath

Widely distributed through the western mountains on rocky slopes from south of Citrusdal to Somerset West and inland on the Witteberg and the Langeberg west of Swellendam

FORM Upright shrub to 1.5m. **LEAVES** 4- to 6-whorled, needle-like, sometimes up to 20mm long, slightly sticky. **FLOWERS** solitary in the upper leaf axils in a head-like cluster near the tops of the stems, short-stalked; bracteoles needle-like. **SEPALS** lance-shaped tapering to a needle-like point, glossy, hairless or minutely hairy, slightly sticky. **COROLLA** tubular, slightly curved, (10–)25–34mm long, hairless or minutely hairy, slightly sticky, orange-red, orange or yellow; lobes slightly spreading, *pointed*. **ANTHERS** 8, concealed or well exserted, *lobes completely separate* and *rounded at the base*. **OVARY** covered with *velvety, down-pointing hairs*. **STYLE** shortly protruding; stigma pinhead.

TWO SUBSPECIES subsp. ***grandiflora*** (= *Erica abietina* subsp. *aurantiaca*) from the Koue Bokkeveld Mtns south of Citrusdal to the Helderberg at Somerset West and east to the Witteberg has yellow-orange to orange-red or bicoloured yellow and red flowers (10–)25–30(–34)mm long; and subsp. ***perfoliosa*** (= *Erica exsurgens*) from Jonkershoek has pure yellow flowers 20–25mm long.

SIMILAR SPECIES *Erica situshiemalis* (= *Erica abietina* subsp. *petraea*) from Groot Winterhoek above Porterville has pure yellow flowers with a velvety, non-sticky corolla 20mm long.

This species now includes all mainland forms previously included in *Erica abietina*.

J	F	M	A	M	J	J	A	S	O	N	D

subsp. *perfoliosa*

James Deacon

subsp. *grandiflora*

Nick Helme

subsp. *grandiflora*

John Manning

Erica thomae `RARE`

Rocky slopes and seepages from Betty's Bay to Kleinmond

FORM Robust upright shrub to 1m. **LEAVES** 6-whorled, suberect-incurved, needle-like. **FLOWERS** solitary in the uppermost leaf axils in a head-like whorl or cluster near the tops of the stems, short-stalked; bracteoles needle-like. **SEPALS** needle-like. **COROLLA** tubular, slightly curved, 20–30mm long, *longitudinally ridged, rather rough-haired like sandpaper, slightly sticky*, pink, reddish, green or white, sometimes bicoloured pink with white tip; lobes slightly spreading, blunt. **ANTHERS** 8, concealed, with *ear-like lobes at the base*. **STYLE** reaching the mouth of the tube; stigma pinhead.

| J | F | M | A | M | J | J | A | S | O | N | D |

Nick Helme

Includes forms previously known as *Erica porteri* and *Erica tenax*.

Erica nevillei `RARE`

Cape Peninsula from Chapman's Peak to Constantiaberg

| J | F | M | A | M | J | J | A | S | O | N | D |

FORM Sprawling or spreading shrub to 30cm. **LEAVES** 4- to 6-whorled, spreading, needle-like, with glands along the margins. **FLOWERS** solitary in the uppermost leaf axils in a cluster at the tips of the stems, stalked; bracteoles needle-like. **SEPALS** lance-shaped tapering to a needle-like point. **COROLLA** tubular and *nipped in or narrowed at the base*, slightly curved, 20–30mm long, longitudinally ribbed at the base, rough-haired like sandpaper, sticky, red; lobes slightly spreading, blunt. **ANTHERS** 8, slightly protruding, *lobes completely separate* and *rounded at the base*. **STYLE** shortly protruding; stigma pinhead.

SIMILAR SPECIES *Erica quadrisulcata* from above Simon's Town on the Cape Peninsula has dull yellow flowers that are flushed orange on the upperside with the corolla longitudinally ribbed at the base.

Anthony Rebelo

Erica viscaria

Flats and lower slopes from Mamre to the Cape Peninsula and eastwards through the Kogelberg and Kleinrivier Mtns to Bredasdorp

FORM Upright shrub to 1m, some forms resprouting from the rootstock. **LEAVES** 4- or 6-whorled, needle-like, finely velvety on both surfaces and with glands along the margins. **FLOWERS** solitary in the upper leaf axils in a short, dense raceme near the tops of the stems, suberect or nodding on short stalks; bracteoles needle-like, with gland-tipped hairs along the lower margins towards the base. **SEPALS** needle-like or more rarely lance-shaped, minutely velvety. **COROLLA** tubular and very slightly constricted at the mouth, *8-ribbed longitudinally*, slightly curved, (5–)12–20mm long, *very minutely bristly, sometimes only along the ribs or towards the base or on the lobes*, dry or slightly sticky, very variable in colour, white, green, yellowish, pink, purple or red, or bicoloured pink with a white mouth or red with a yellow mouth; lobes slightly spreading, blunt. **ANTHERS** 8, deeply concealed in short-flowered forms but reaching just below the mouth of the corolla tube in longer-flowered forms, rounded or toothed at the base. **OVARY** *covered with long white hairs*. **STYLE** concealed or reaching just beyond the mouth of the corolla; stigma pinhead. (See p. 104 for *Erica viscaria* subsp. *viscaria*.)

Includes forms previously known as *Erica decora, Erica gallorum, Erica longifolia* and *Erica onosmiflora.*

| J | F | M | A | M | J | J | A | S | O | N | D |

SIX SUBSPECIES subsp. *viscaria* from the Cape Peninsula and surrounding flats has short flowers 5–9mm long; subsp. *longifolia* (= *Erica longifolia*) has variably coloured flowers 12–20mm long and very narrow bract, bracteoles and sepals; subsp. *macrosepala* (= *Erica onosmiflora*) from the Kleinrivier Mtns has yellowish to green or rarely white flowers with more leaf-shaped sepals; subsp. *gallorum* (= *Erica gallorum*) from near Elgin has short flowers 5–10(–12)mm long, either pinkish throughout or bicoloured pink below and white above; subsp. *pustulata* (= *Erica pustulata*) from the Kleinrivier Mtns has short, markedly pustulate yellow flowers 7mm long; and subsp. *pendula* from the eastern end of the Paardeberg between Kleinmond and Bot River Village, has pendulous white flowers 12–18mm long.

subsp. *macrosepala*

subsp. *gallorum*

subsp. *longifolia*

Nick Helme

subsp. *longifolia*

Ross Turner

subsp. *longifolia*

Ross Turner

subsp. *longifolia*

Ross Turner

subsp. *pendula*

Ross Turner

Erica vestita

Trembling Heath, Wide-mouthed Heath, Trilheide

Riviersonderend Mtns and the Langeberg south to Agulhas

FORM Upright shrub to 1m, densely leafy. **LEAVES** 6-whorled, needle-like or *thread-like, often to 20mm* long, finely velvety on the upper surface and margins, with *slender, sticky petioles*. **FLOWERS** solitary in the upper leaf axils in a short, dense, sometimes interrupted raceme near the tops of the stems, suberect on short stalks; bracteoles needle-like. **SEPALS** needle-like but widened and lance-shaped at the base, and *velvety*. **COROLLA** tubular, slightly curved, 16–25mm long, *finely hairy or velvety*, white, pink or purple to red; lobes slightly spreading, blunt. **ANTHERS** 8, reaching mouth of corolla tube or shortly exserted, rounded or toothed at the base. **STYLE** shortly protruding; stigma pinhead.

John Manning

| J | F | M | A | M | J | J | A | S | O | N | D |

Ross Turner

John Manning

Erica pinea

Bain's Kloof along the Hottentots
Holland Mtns to the Kleinrivier Mtns

FORM Upright shrub to 1.5m.
LEAVES 6-whorled, spreading-incurved
to suberect, needle-like, *sometimes
to 20mm* long, minutely hairy on both
surfaces. **FLOWERS** solitary in the upper
leaf axils forming a raceme near the tops
of the stems, suberect on short stalks;
bracteoles needle-like, pressed against the
calyx. **SEPALS** needle-like but widened and
lance-shaped at the base. **COROLLA** tubular,
slightly curved, 20–24mm long, *hairless*,
white or bicoloured pale yellow with white
tips, rarely purplish pink; lobes slightly
spreading, blunt. **ANTHERS** 8, reaching
mouth of corolla tube or shortly exserted,
short-spurred at the base. **OVARY** *hairless,
6- to 8-chambered*. **STYLE** shortly
protruding; stigma pinhead.

Ross Turner

| J | F | M | A | M | J | J | A | S | O | N | D |

John Manning

Anthony Rebelo

Erica regia ENDANGERED

Elim Heath

Sandy or gravelly flats and limestone hills from Bredasdorp to Still Bay

FORM Upright or straggling shrub to 2m.
LEAVES 6-whorled, needle-like, sometimes minutely hairy, with glands along the margins.
FLOWERS solitary in the upper leaf axils in a whorl near the tops of the stems, on short stalks; bracteoles needle-like. **SEPALS** lance-shaped, hard and glossy. **COROLLA** tubular, not or only slightly constricted at the mouth, 14–20mm long, *hairless* and *slightly sticky*, red or white or variegated pink with white base and red tip; lobes spreading, blunt. **ANTHERS** 8, concealed in corolla tube, with a *slight chin at the base* and *short-spurred*. **OVARY** with *erect hairs on top*. **STYLE** reaching the mouth of the tube; stigma pinhead.

J | F | M | A | M | J | J | A | S | O | N | D

> **TWO SUBSPECIES** subsp. *regia* has the corolla constricted at the mouth; and subsp. *mariae* has the corolla not constricted at the mouth.

> This species now includes white-flowered forms previously recognised as *Erica casta* as well as plants from limestone outcrops between Bredasdorp and Still Bay previously recognised as *Erica mariae* that do not have the corolla tube nipped in at the tip.

Ismail Ebrahim

subsp. *regia*

subsp. *mariae*

Nick Helme

Erica fascicularis

Fascicled Heath

Helderberg to the Riviersonderend Mtns to Bredasdorp

J | F | M | A | M | J | J | A | S | O | N | D

FORM Upright, sometimes wand-like or willowy shrub to 2m. **LEAVES** 6-whorled, arching outward, needle-like, *12–15mm long*, minutely velvety on the upper surface with glandular margins. **FLOWERS** solitary in the uppermost leaf axils clustered in a head or whorl at the branch tips, *spreading on long stalks*; bracteoles needle-like. **SEPALS** narrowly lance-shaped, sticky. **COROLLA** tubular and sometimes slightly swollen at the top, slightly curved, 25–30mm long, hairless, smooth below but rough and sandpaper-like in the upper part, *very sticky, rosy pink but paler above* and with *green lobes*; lobes suberect, pointed. **ANTHERS** concealed, *tailed or horned at the base*. **STYLE** reaching the mouth of the tube or just beyond; stigma pinhead.

Ross Turner

Erica massonii

Firewheel Heath

Hottentots Holland to Kleinrivier Mtns

FORM Upright, sometimes wand-like shrublet to 1m. **LEAVES** 4- to 6-whorled, arching outward, needle-like, *2–7mm* long, hairless or minutely velvety on the upper surface towards the ends, with *long bristles along the slightly thickened margins and on the underside*. **FLOWERS** solitary in the uppermost leaf axils *clustered in a flat whorl at the branch tips, spreading on bristly stalks*; bracteoles needle-like, with long bristles. **SEPALS** narrowly lance-shaped, *covered with long bristles in the outer half*. **COROLLA** narrowly urn-shaped and slightly swollen at the top, slightly curved, 25mm long, hairless, *very sticky, bright glossy red with a pale green tip* and *darker green lobes*; lobes erect, pointed. **ANTHERS** concealed, *rounded at the base* with the *filaments widened at the top*. **STYLE** reaching the mouth of the tube or just beyond; stigma pinhead.

J | F | M | A | M | J | J | A | S | O | N | D

Ross Turner

Nick Helme

Cluster 6 ■ VELVETY TRUMPET HEATHS

Flowers at the tips of individual short side-shoots, sometimes aggregated in false-spikes or -racemes towards the ends of the stems, with a velvety or finely hairy corolla

Erica conspicua
Conspicuous Heath

Usually in seepages or along streams from Ceres to Franschhoek and Hex River Mtns

FORM Upright shrub to 1.8m, with numerous short-shoots. **LEAVES** 4-whorled, needle-like, *velvety with longer hairs along the margins*. **FLOWERS** usually solitary at the tips of short-shoots aggregated in clusters or loose false-racemes towards the ends of the branches, stalked; bracteoles needle-like. **SEPALS** lance-shaped, *hard* and *glossy* with a *wide groove down the centre, fringed with hairs along the margins*. **COROLLA** tubular and flaring at the mouth, curved, mostly 24–36mm long, velvety or finely hairy, sulphur-yellow to orange; lobes slightly spreading, blunt. **ANTHERS** 8, visible or shortly protruding, *rounded at the base, which is curved forwards like a chin*. **STYLE** shortly protruding; stigma pinhead.

Distinguished from the very similar *Erica curviflora* (opposite) by the mostly larger flowers and hard, glossy sepals with a wide median groove. The two species may grow together, and hybrids between them have been recorded.

| J | F | M | A | M | J | J | A | S | O | N | D |

TWO SUBSPECIES subsp. *conspicua* from Ceres to Franschhoek has orange flowers 24–36mm long; and subsp. *roseoflora* from east of Worcester to Robertson has pale pink flowers 8–15mm long.

John Manning

subsp. *conspicua*

Ross Turner

subsp. *conspicua*

Ross Turner

subsp. *conspicua*

Erica curviflora

Showy Water Heath, Waterbos

Widespread from near Nieuwoudtville to the Cape Peninsula and east to Makhanda, usually in seepages or along streams

FORM Upright shrub to 1.8m, with numerous short-shoots. **LEAVES** 4-whorled, needle-like, hairless or finely velvety. **FLOWERS** solitary or in pairs at the tips of short-shoots aggregated in loose false-racemes towards the ends of the branches, stalked; bracteoles needle-like. **SEPALS** needle-like or lance-shaped, hairless or velvety. **COROLLA** tubular and flaring at the mouth, curved, 20–30mm long, velvety or finely hairy, *pink to orange or red*, paler at the tips; lobes slightly spreading, blunt. **ANTHERS** 8, visible or shortly protruding, rounded at the base. **OVARY** *distinctly warty*. **STYLE** shortly protruding; stigma pinhead.

Distinguished from the very similar *Erica conspicua* (opposite) by the mostly smaller flowers and finely grooved sepals. The two species may grow together, and hybrids between them have been recorded.

| J | F | M | A | M | J | J | A | S | O | N | D |

Erica stagnalis

Yellow Water Heath

Seepages or along streams from Franschhoek to Hottentots Holland Mtns

| J | F | M | A | M | J | J | A | S | O | N | D |

FORM Upright shrub to 1.5m, with numerous short-shoots. **LEAVES** 4-whorled, needle-like, finely velvety. **FLOWERS** solitary at the tips of short-shoots aggregated in loose false-racemes towards the ends of the branches, stalked; bracteoles needle-like. **SEPALS** lance-shaped, velvety. **COROLLA** tubular and flaring at the mouth, curved, 12–24mm long, hairy, *bright yellow*; lobes slightly spreading, blunt. **ANTHERS** 8, visible or shortly protruding, rounded at the base. **OVARY** *8-chambered*. **STYLE** shortly protruding; stigma pinhead.

Erica perspicua

Prince of Wales Heath, Veerheide

Coastal marshes and vleis from Betty's Bay to Hermanus

FORM Upright shrub with leafy stems to 2m. **LEAVES** 3- or 4-whorled on short-shoots that are also whorled on the stem, needle-like and *4.5mm* long. **FLOWERS** suberect and solitary at the tips of the short-shoots, aggregated in dense and often long false-spikes in the upper part of the stem and branches, ±stalkless; bracteoles needle-like. **SEPALS** lance-shaped. **COROLLA** tubular and flaring slightly at the mouth, straight, *20–22mm* long, velvety or finely hairy, *white or pink to almost purple, often somewhat bicoloured*; lobes slightly spreading, rounded. **ANTHERS** 8, concealed, *spurred at the base*. **OVARY** *8-chambered*. **STYLE** reaching the mouth of the tube; stigma pinhead.

Similar to *Erica colorans* (see p. 78), from Stanford to Elim, which has slightly dumbell-shaped flowers with an almost imperceptible 'waist' and a mostly 6-chambered ovary.

J	F	M	A	M	J	J	A	S	O	N	D

TWO SUBSPECIES subsp. *perspicua* from Rooi Els to Kleinmond has shaggy hairs at the back of the anthers; and subsp. *latifolia* from Hermanus to Stanford has hairless anthers.

Helen Pickering

subsp. *perspicua*

Ross Turner

John Manning

subsp. *perspicua*

subsp. *perspicua*

Erica macowanii

Moist marshy conditions on mountain slopes from the Kogelberg to the Kleinrivier Mtns and Caledon Swartberg

FORM Upright or willowy shrub to 1.2m, with numerous short-shoots. **LEAVES** 4-whorled, needle-like. **FLOWERS** solitary at the tips of short-shoots aggregated in loose false-spikes towards the ends of the branches, ±stalkless; bracteoles lance-shaped. **SEPALS** *lance-shaped* and *papery*. **COROLLA** tubular and flaring at the mouth, straight, 22–25mm long, velvety, yellow or bicoloured red or pink with yellow or white tips, or plain pink or yellow; lobes slightly spreading, blunt. **ANTHERS** 8, visible or shortly protruding, *spurred at the base*. **OVARY** *8-chambered*. **STYLE** shortly protruding; stigma pinhead.

| J | F | M | A | M | J | J | A | S | O | N | D |

TWO SUBSPECIES subsp. *macowanii* from the Kogelberg has elliptical sepals and a finely velvety corolla; and subsp. *lanceolata* from the Kleinrivier Mtns has narrower, lance-shaped sepals and a more shaggy corolla.

SIMILAR SPECIES *Erica leucotrachela*, also from damp slopes and seepages on the Kogelberg and the Kleinrivier Mtns, has shorter flowers with a somewhat club-shaped corolla 16–18mm long that bulges slightly below the mouth and is bicoloured pink to purple with a white tip.

subsp. *macowanii*

Nick Helme

Erica densifolia

Langeberg to the Kammanassie and Tsitsikamma Mtns

| J | F | M | A | M | J | J | A | S | O | N | D |

FORM Upright shrublet with stems to 90cm, closely covered with short-shoots. **LEAVES** densely 4-whorled on short-shoots, small and needle-like, shiny and sticky. **FLOWERS** solitary at the tips of the short-shoots, aggregated in dense false-spikes in the upper part of the stem and branches, ±stalkless; bracteoles needle-like. **SEPALS** lance-shaped. **COROLLA** tubular and flaring at the mouth, curved, 24–30mm long, finely hairy and *slightly sticky, bicoloured pink to red with green tips*; lobes slightly spreading, rounded. **ANTHERS** 8, concealed, *long-horned at the base*. **STYLE** shortly protruding; stigma pinhead.

Nick Helme

Erica verticillata `EXTINCT` Whorled Heath

Seasonally damp sandy flats on the Cape Peninsula from Black River to Zeekoevlei
FORM Upright shrub with wand-like stems to 1.5m, with numerous short-shoots.
LEAVES 4- to 6-whorled, needle-like. **FLOWERS** *mostly in 4s at the tips of short-shoots*,
aggregated in clusters or short interrupted false-spikes, short-stalked; bracteoles needle-
like. **SEPALS** needle-like. **COROLLA** tubular, slightly curved, 15–20mm long, finely hairy,
mauve-pink; lobes spreading, blunt. **ANTHERS** 8, concealed, *spurred at the base*.
OVARY *8-chambered*, with *erect calluses at the top*. **STYLE** reaching the mouth of the
tube; stigma pinhead.

> This species was extinct in the wild by 1950.
> Plants derived from cultivated material have since
> been reintroduced to selected conservation areas
> on the Cape Peninsula, but it remains to be seen
> if any of these introductions establish themselves.

| J | F | M | A | M | J | J | A | S | O | N | D |

Erica pillansii `RARE`

Coastal marshes and in seeps on the Kogelberg, near the mouth of the Palmiet River

FORM Upright shrub with wand-like stems to 1.2m, closely covered with short-shoots.
LEAVES densely 4-whorled on short-shoots, needle-like, minutely hairy. **FLOWERS** 1 to 3 at the tips of short-shoots, aggregated in false-spikes, short-stalked; bracteoles needle-like.
SEPALS lance-shaped, velvety, with sticky glands along the margins. **COROLLA** tubular, slightly curved, *7–15mm* long, velvety, *blood-red*; lobes slightly spreading, blunt.
ANTHERS 8, concealed, *spurred at the base*. **STYLE** reaching the mouth of the tube; stigma pinhead.

Now includes smaller-flowered forms previously recognised as the separate species *Erica fervida*.

J F M A M J J A S O N D

TWO SUBSPECIES subsp. *pillansii* has flowers 12–16mm long in long false-spikes 12–26cm long; and subsp. *fervida* has flowers 6–10mm long in shorter false-spikes 6–12cm long.

subsp. *pillansii*

Anthony Rebelo

Cluster 7 ■ SMOOTH OR STICKY TRUMPET HEATHS

Flowers at the tips of individual short side-shoots, sometimes aggregated in false-spikes or -racemes towards the ends of the stems, with a hairless (rarely with scattered gland-tipped hairs), smooth or sometimes sticky corolla

Erica annectens VULNERABLE

Clinging Heath

Cape Peninsula above Kalk Bay

FORM Upright to spreading shrub to 1m, with numerous short-shoots. **LEAVES** 4- to 6-whorled, spreading, needle-like. **FLOWERS** solitary in the uppermost leaf axils of the short-shoots, thus apparently in 4s, clustered into false-racemes, short-stalked; bracteoles needle-like. **SEPALS** lance-shaped and papery at base with needle-like tips. **COROLLA** tubular, slightly curved, *20–24mm* long, hairless, *dull orange* but *lobes and lower surface paler yellow*; lobes spreading, blunt. **ANTHERS** 8, concealed, lobes completely separate and *rounded at the base* with *crook-shaped filaments*. **OVARY** 8-chambered. **STYLE** reaching the mouth of the tube or just beyond; stigma pinhead.

| J | F | M | A | M | J | J | A | S | O | N | D |

Corinne Merry

Erica patersonii `ENDANGERED`   Mealie Heath, Mielieheide

Coastal marshy flats at Cape Point and from Betty's Bay to Stanford

FORM Stiffly erect shrublet with leafy, rod-like stems to 1m. **LEAVES** densely 4-whorled in tufts on short-shoots that are whorled on the stem, curved inwards, needle-like. **FLOWERS** solitary at the tips of the short-shoots aggregated in a *dense false-spike in the upper part of the stem, ±stalkless*; bracteoles needle-like. **SEPALS** lance-shaped with *slender needle-like tips*. **COROLLA** tubular, *14–18mm* long, hairless, *yellow*; lobes erect, rounded. **ANTHERS** 8, concealed, long-horned at the base. **STYLE** concealed; stigma pinhead.

This species was formerly incorrectly spelled *Erica pattersonia*.

J | F | M | A | M | J | J | A | S | O | N | D

Ross Turner

Ross Turner

John Manning

Erica maximiliani

Max Schlechter's Heath, Bedrock Heath

Drier, rocky mountain slopes, often in rock crevices, from the Cederberg through the Koue Bokkeveld to the Witteberg and the mountains around Ladismith

FORM Spreading or upright shrublet to 80cm, with numerous short-shoots. **LEAVES** 4-whorled, needle-like, finely velvety on the upper surface and with *minute fine wispy hairs along the margins when young*. **FLOWERS** 1 to 4 at the tips of short-shoots aggregated in loose clusters at the ends of the branches, stalked; bracteoles needle-like. **SEPALS** lance-shaped, with fringed margins. **COROLLA** tubular, straight or curved, *28–33mm* long, hairless, *pale green to pale yellow*; lobes slightly spreading, rounded. **ANTHERS** 8, concealed, horned at the base. **STYLE** shortly protruding; stigma pinhead.

John Manning

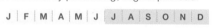

| J | F | M | A | M | J | J | A | S | O | N | D |

Nick Helme

John Manning

Erica discolor

Betty's Bay along the coastal ranges to Humansdorp and inland on the Witteberg and Swartberg

Includes forms previously known as *Erica hebecalyx* and *Erica speciosa*.

FORM Upright shrub with leafy stems to 2m. **LEAVES** densely *3-whorled* on short-shoots, needle-like, shiny and sticky. **FLOWERS** solitary at the tips of the short-shoots aggregated in short or long false-spikes in the upper part of the stem and branches, ±stalkless; bracteoles needle-like. **SEPALS** lance-shaped. **COROLLA** tubular and flaring at the mouth, curved, 18–24mm long, hairless, plain pink to red or bicoloured with yellow or white tips; lobes slightly spreading, rounded. **ANTHERS** 8, concealed, *long-horned at the base*. **STYLE** shortly protruding; stigma pinhead.

J	F	M	A	M	J	J	A	S	O	N	D

Nick Helme

John Manning

Ross Turner

John Manning

Erica versicolor

Varicoloured Heath, Two-tone Heath

Cederberg through the Koue Bokkeveld
to the Anysberg, and along the
Langeberg and foothills to Mossel Bay

J	F	M	A	M	J	J	A	S	O	N	D

Very similar to **Erica discolor** (although
the leaves are sometimes 4-whorled) but
the *tips of the sepals are narrowed
above* to resemble the needle-like leaves,
the *stamen filaments* are *widened* and
spoon-like at the base, and the *anthers*
are only *very shortly spurred* at the base.

Erica unicolor

Unicoloured Heath

Outeniqua Mtns

FORM Upright shrub with leafy stems to 1.5m. **LEAVES** densely *4-whorled* on short-shoots,
needle-like, hairless or hairy. **FLOWERS** solitary at the tips of the short-shoots aggregated in short
or long false-spikes in the upper part of the stem and branches, ±stalkless; bracteoles needle-
like. **SEPALS** lance-shaped below, with *needle-like
tips*. **COROLLA** tubular and flaring at the mouth,
curved, 16–22mm long, hairless, *plain green or
bicoloured red at base with green tips*;
lobes slightly spreading, rounded. **ANTHERS** 8,
concealed, rounded or horned at the base.
STYLE shortly protruding; stigma pinhead.

Includes forms previously known as
Erica dichrus and *Erica viridescens*.

J	F	M	A	M	J	J	A	S	O	N	D

THREE SUBSPECIES subsp. *unicolor*
from the southern slopes has longer leaves
6–10mm long and unicoloured yellow-
green flowers (previously *Erica viridescens*);
subsp. *mutica* from the lowlands has
shorter leaves 5–6mm long and bicoloured
flowers red with green tips (previously *Erica
dichrus*); and subsp. *georgica* from near
George has longer leaves 7–11mm long
and bicoloured flowers red or pink with
green or yellow tips.

subsp. *unicolor*

Erica diaphana
Diaphanous Heath

Flats and rocky slopes on the Outeniqua and Tsitsikamma Mtns to Kariega

FORM Upright shrub with wand-like stems to 1.8m, with numerous short-shoots. **LEAVES** *3-whorled*, needle-like. **FLOWERS** mostly in 3s at the tips of short-shoots, nodding, stalked; bracteoles lance-shaped, clasping the calyx, sticky. **SEPALS** lance-shaped, *sticky*. **COROLLA** tubular and slightly swollen at the mouth, straight, 20–24mm long, hairless and *very sticky*, pale pink to purplish with greenish tip; lobes slightly spreading, blunt. **ANTHERS** 8, concealed, *rounded or minutely spurred* with a chin-like protrusion at the base. **STYLE** shortly protruding; stigma pinhead.

J	F	M	A	M	J	J	A	S	O	N	D

Ross Turner

Erica glandulosa
Glandular Heath

Flats and lower slopes along the southern coast and mountains from Mossel Bay to Gqeberha and inland through the Baviaanskloof Mtns to the eastern Swartberg

FORM Upright shrub to 1.8m, with numerous short-shoots; the stems are densely covered with gland-tipped bristles. **LEAVES** *4-whorled*, spreading, needle-like, *densely covered with gland-tipped bristles*. **FLOWERS** 2 to 5 at the tips of short-shoots aggregated in loose false-racemes towards the ends of the branches, stalked; *bracteoles needle-like, pressed against the calyx*, densely covered with gland-tipped bristles. **SEPALS** needle-like, *densely covered with gland-tipped bristles*. **COROLLA** tubular and flaring at the mouth, curved, 18–32mm long, hairless or with scattered gland-tipped hairs, *pink or orange with marked red veins*; lobes slightly spreading, blunt. **ANTHERS** 8, visible or shortly protruding, rounded at the base, which is curved forwards like a chin. **STYLE** shortly protruding; stigma pinhead.

Includes forms previously known as *Erica fourcadei*.

J	F	M	A	M	J	J	A	S	O	N	D

FOUR SUBSPECIES subsp. *glandulosa* has needle-like leaves 5–7mm long and flowers 20–30mm long; subsp. *fourcadei* from the coast between Sedgefield and Kareedouw has broader leaves 7–10mm long and flowers 20–30mm long (previously *Erica fourcadei*); subsp. *bondiae* from the Kammanassie Mtns to Haarlem has needle-like leaves and shorter hairless flowers 10mm long (previously *Erica bondiae*); and subsp. *breviflora* from northwest of Humansdorp has needle-like leaves and glandular-haired flowers 10mm long.

Ross Turner

subsp. *glandulosa*

Erica viridiflora

Swartberg and Outeniqua Mtns to
Humansdorp

J | F | M | A | M | J | J | A | S | O | N | D

FORM Erect, untidy shrublet to 1m.
LEAVES 3-whorled, needle-like. **FLOWERS** in
nodding 3-flowered heads at the tips of
the branches, stalked; bracteoles lance-
shaped, clasping the calyx. **SEPALS** lance-
shaped. **COROLLA** tubular, 18–26mm
long (only 5mm long in subsp. *redacta*),
hairless and usually *sticky, lime-green;*
lobes erect, pointed. **ANTHERS** 8,
concealed, with *short spurs or teeth at*
the base partly joined to the filaments.
STYLE shortly protruding; stigma pinhead.

THREE SUBSPECIES subsp. *viridiflora*
from the coastal mountains has sticky,
lime-green flowers 22–26mm long;
subsp. *primulina* from the Swartberg Mtns
has paler, cream-coloured to greenish, non-
sticky flowers 18–20mm long (previously
Erica primulina); and subsp. *redacta* from
Meiringspoort in the Swartberg Mtns differs
from subsp. *primulina* in its much smaller
flowers 5mm long.

subsp. *viridiflora*

subsp. *viridiflora*

Erica colorans VULNERABLE

Blushing Heath, Tregterheide

Coastal marshes and vleis from Stanford to Elim

FORM Upright shrub with leafy stems to 1.8m. **LEAVES** 4-whorled on short-shoots that are whorled on the stem, needle-like. **FLOWERS** spreading or slightly nodding, 1 to 4 at the tips of the short-shoots aggregated in false-spikes in the upper part of the stem and branches, ±stalkless; bracteoles needle-like. **SEPALS** lance-shaped. **COROLLA** tubular and *swollen slightly below the mouth, which is slightly constricted, straight, 14–16mm* long, hairless, *white flushed pink*; lobes slightly spreading, rounded. **ANTHERS** 8, concealed, *black, rounded at the base* or with *minute horns partially joined to the filaments*. **STYLE** shortly protruding; stigma pinhead.

| J | F | M | A | M | J | J | A | S | O | N | D |

Ross Turner

Erica cruenta

Crimson Heath, Rooiheide

Clay flats and slopes from Grabouw through the southern foothills of the Overberg to Mossel Bay

FORM Upright shrub with wand-like stems to 1.5m, closely covered with short-shoots. **LEAVES** densely 3-whorled on short-shoots, needle-like. **FLOWERS** 1 to 3 at the tips of short-shoots, aggregated in false-racemes, stalked; bracteoles needle-like. **SEPALS** lance-shaped, with *sticky glands along the margins*. **COROLLA** tubular, slightly curved, 20–22mm long, hairless, *blood-red*; lobes spreading, blunt. **ANTHERS** 8, concealed, *horned at the base*. **STYLE** reaching the mouth of the tube; stigma pinhead.

Klaus Wehrlin

| J | F | M | A | M | J | J | A | S | O | N | D |

Erica inordinata `RARE` Fiery Heath

At high altitudes on rocky southern slopes of the Kammanassie Mtns

FORM Upright shrub with wand-like stems to 1.2m, closely covered with short-shoots. **LEAVES** densely 3-whorled on short-shoots, scale-like, minutely hairy. **FLOWERS** solitary at the tips of upper short-shoots, aggregated in short or long false-spikes towards the ends of the branches, spreading, stalked; bracteoles leaf-shaped, sometimes the inner pair narrower and awl-shaped, firm and sticky. **SEPALS** lance-shaped, *firm-textured*, with the *margins curled inwards, glossy* and *very sticky, red when fresh*, turning straw-coloured. **COROLLA** broadly tubular and *slightly narrowed in the middle* like a dumbbell, *becoming markedly swollen in some flowers, abruptly constricted around the small mouth*, 15–25mm long, hairless and *very sticky*, blood-red; lobes erect or slightly spreading above, blunt. **ANTHERS** 8, concealed, spurred at the base. **STYLE** protruding shortly beyond the mouth of the tube; stigma pinhead.

| J | F | M | A | M | J | J | A | S | O | N | D |

Erica chloroloma `VULNERABLE` Green-tipped Heath

Coastal limestone formations from Wilderness to Fish River Mouth

FORM Upright shrub to 2.5m. **LEAVES** 4- to 6-whorled on stems, needle-like, minutely hairy. **FLOWERS** mostly 3 or 4 at the tips of branchlets, sometimes aggregated in larger whorls, stalked; bracteoles needle-like. **SEPALS** lance-shaped, widened towards the base with somewhat membranous margins, *fringed and hairy along the margins*, especially towards the base, with glands. **COROLLA** tubular, 14–16mm long, hairless, *red with green lobes*; lobes erect, blunt. **ANTHERS** 8, concealed, *horned at the base*. **STYLE** reaching the mouth of the tube; stigma pinhead.

| J | F | M | A | M | J | J | A | S | O | N | D |

GROUP 2
VASE HEATHS

Flowers with a straight, vase-shaped or very narrowly tubular corolla, with a small, pinhole mouth and recurved or spreading star-like lobes, often pink with a dark throat or ring around the mouth

Cluster 1 ■ CLAMMY HORSEFLY HEATHS

Stems and leaves covered with long, gland-tipped, tentacle-like hairs, the flowers medium to large with a hairy corolla 8–24mm long, sharply constricted round the mouth like a drawstring

Erica glandulifera

Dewy Heath

Along the western mountains from the Koue Bokkeveld Mtns above Ceres to the Groot Winterhoek Mtns above Tulbagh

FORM Sprawling shrublet 45cm, with erect flowering stems bearing closely leafy short-shoots in the lower leaf axils; the reddish stems are covered with gland-tipped, tentacle-like hairs. **LEAVES** mostly scattered or 3-whorled, spreading at right angles to the stem, needle-like, velvety and with long, gland-tipped, tentacle-like hairs on the lower surface and along the margins. **FLOWERS** *solitary in the upper axils in well-separated whorls of 1 to 3 flowers* forming a very loose raceme at the branch tips, erect or slightly nodding on short or long stalks that are covered with soft hairs mixed with long, gland-tipped, tentacle-like hairs; bracteoles needle-like or lance-shaped, velvety and with long, gland-tipped, tentacle-like hairs. **SEPALS** needle-like or lance-shaped, covered with *long, gland-tipped tentacle-like hairs*. **COROLLA** urn-shaped and noticeably contracted around the small mouth, *12–24mm* long, velvety, sticky, pale pink below with a dark reddish band around the top of the tube; lobes curling backwards, rounded. **ANTHERS** 8, concealed, with red crests at the base. **STYLE** protruding just beyond the mouth of the tube; stigma pinhead.

Includes plants previously known as *Erica irrorata*.

| J | F | M | A | M | J | J | A | S | O | N | D |

Ross Turner

Erica glutinosa

Clammy Heath

Damp sandy areas and seepages on slopes of the southwestern mountains from Ceres to the Hottentots Holland Mtns and the Cape Peninsula and shortly eastwards onto the Babilonstoring and Riviersonderend Mtns

FORM Upright shrublet 30cm, with flowering stems sometimes bearing additional flowering branchlets; the reddish stems are covered with gland-tipped, tentacle-like hairs. **LEAVES** mostly scattered and not evidently whorled, spreading at right angles to the stem, needle-like, velvety and with long, gland-tipped, tentacle-like hairs on the lower surface and along the margins. **FLOWERS** in *loose rounded clusters or short racemes at the branch tips*, erect or slightly nodding on long slender stalks that are covered with soft hairs mixed with long, gland-tipped, tentacle-like hairs; bracteoles scale-like. **SEPALS** lance-shaped, *firm and glossy, hairless*. **COROLLA** urn-shaped and noticeably contracted around the small mouth, *8–10mm* long, velvety, sticky, pale pink below with a dark reddish band around the top of the tube; lobes curling backwards, rounded. **ANTHERS** 8, concealed, crested at the base. **STYLE** protruding just beyond the mouth of the tube; stigma pinhead.

| J | F | M | A | M | J | J | A | S | O | N | D |

Nick Helme

Cluster 2 ■ LARGE HORSEFLY HEATHS

Larger-flowered species with a hairless corolla 10mm or more long, either sharply constricted round the mouth like a drawstring or tapering smoothly

Erica embothriifolia

Firebush-leaved Heath

Riviersonderend Mtns

J	F	M	A	M	J	J	A	S	O	N	D

FORM Sparse, upright or sprawling shrublet to 30cm; with slender stems covered with short, gland-tipped hairs. **LEAVES** rather distantly 3-whorled, *spreading at right angles to the stem*, needle-like, mostly 10mm long, minutely velvety on the upper surface and with scattered gland-tipped hairs, especially towards the tips, and with *long, whisker-like bristles along the margins*. **FLOWERS** clustered in a whorl at the branch tips on long, slender, sticky, hairless stalks; bracteoles scale-like, sticky. **SEPALS** lance-shaped, *hard and glossy, sticky*, in two slightly unequal pairs with the outer pair slightly larger and with a short or

Nick Helme

long, gland-tipped bristle at the tip. **COROLLA** tubular and cylindrical or club-shaped, sharply constricted at the mouth, 12–24mm long, hairless, slightly sticky, bright pink with a dark purple ring around the throat; lobes curling backwards, rounded. **ANTHERS** 8, *completely protruding* and *joined along the margins in a tight collar around the style*, with *long, bristle-like tails* at the base. **STYLE** protruding well beyond the anthers; stigma pinhead.

Erica gysbertii

Gysbert's Heath

Kogelberg Biosphere Reserve and Hangklip

J	F	M	A	M	J	J	A	S	O	N	D

FORM Upright rounded shrublet to 90cm. **LEAVES** 4-whorled, needle-like, *fringed with long bristles* that break off with age. **FLOWERS** clustered in a whorl at the branch tips, on short stalks; bracteoles lance-shaped, bristly. **SEPALS** lance-shaped with *long, reddish bristles*. **COROLLA** vase-shaped and sharply constricted at the throat, 10–15mm long, hairless, slightly sticky, pink to red with a dark ring around the throat; lobes spreading and pointed. **ANTHERS** 8, concealed, *short, covered with short wispy hairs*, with a notched chin-like protuberance at the base. **STYLE** reaching the mouth of the tube; stigma pinhead.

Nick Helme

Erica aristata

Kleinrivier Mtns

FORM Upright shrublet to 70cm. **LEAVES** 4-whorled, *arching outwards, elliptical*, with *minute prickles along the margins* and *shortly pointed* at the tip. **FLOWERS** clustered in a whorl at the branch tips, on short stalks; bracteoles lance-shaped. **SEPALS** lance-shaped, sticky. **COROLLA** narrowly vase-shaped and constricted at the throat, 25–30mm long, hairless, sticky, pale pink but darker around the throat and base with fine dark lines along the tube; lobes spreading and *rounded, slightly frilled*. **ANTHERS** 8, slightly protruding, with a rough chin-like protuberance at the base. **STYLE** reaching the mouth of the tube; stigma pinhead.

| J | F | M | A | M | J | J | A | S | O | N | D |

Christopher Whitehouse

Erica retorta

Flats and lower slopes from Villiersdorp to Betty's Bay

| J | F | M | A | M | J | J | A | S | O | N | D |

FORM Spreading shrublet to 60cm. **LEAVES** 4-whorled, *arching outwards*, elliptical, with *minute prickles* along the margins, *tipped with a long red bristle*. **FLOWERS** clustered in a whorl at the branch tips, stalked; bracteoles lance-shaped and bristle-tipped. **SEPALS** lance-shaped and *bristle-tipped*, sticky. **COROLLA** narrowly vase-shaped and constricted at the throat, 10–20mm long, hairless, sticky, pale to dark pink but darker around the throat with fine dark lines along the tube; lobes spreading and pointed. **ANTHERS** 8, concealed, with a silky and chin-like protuberance at the base. **STYLE** reaching the mouth of the tube; stigma pinhead.

Nick Helme

Erica jasminiflora `CRITICALLY ENDANGERED`   Jasmine Heath, Trompetheide

Very rare, in renosterveld shrubland on lower slopes and known only from Shaw's Pass and the northern foothills of the Kleinrivier Mtns near Caledon

FORM Slender willowy shrublet to 60cm, with short spreading branchlets. **LEAVES** 3-whorled, needle-like. **FLOWERS** in clusters of 3 or 4 at the branch tips, stalked; bracteoles lance-shaped. **SEPALS** lance-shaped. **COROLLA** *narrowly tubular* and *constricted at the throat*, 30–32mm long, hairless, pale pink; lobes conspicuous and spreading, pointed. **ANTHERS** 8, concealed, with a rough chin-like protuberance at the base. **STYLE** reaching the mouth of the tube; stigma pinhead.

J | F | M | A | M | J | J | A | S | O | N | D

Ismail Ebrahim

Ismail Ebrahim

Ismail Ebrahim

Erica junonia

Cederberg to the Hex River Mtns

J | F | M | A | M | J | J | A | S | O | N | D

FORM Upright or sprawling shrublet to 50cm. **LEAVES** 3-whorled, needle-like. **FLOWERS** clustered at the branch tips, stalked; bracteoles lance-shaped. **SEPALS** lance-shaped. **COROLLA** vase-shaped with a swollen base and *narrow neck that bulges at the top* and is *constricted at the throat*, 18–50mm long, hairless, pink; lobes conspicuous and spreading, pointed. **ANTHERS** 8, concealed, with a rough chin-like protuberance at the base and *shortly awned*. **STYLE** reaching the mouth of the tube; stigma pinhead.

Erica ampullacea

Lower mountain slopes and limestone hills from Caledon to Bredasdorp

FORM Upright or straggling shrublet to 60cm. **LEAVES** *4-whorled*, needle-like. **FLOWERS** in heads of 3 or 4 at the branch tips, on short stalks; bracteoles enlarged, lance-shaped, almost clasping the sepals. **SEPALS** enlarged and lance-shaped, fringed. **COROLLA** *vase-shaped* with a *swollen base* and *narrow, fluted neck constricted at the throat*, 18–24mm long, hairless, white with pink blotches in the mouth; lobes conspicuous and spreading, rounded. **ANTHERS** 8, concealed, with a rough chin-like protuberance at the base and *shortly awned*. **STYLE** reaching the mouth of the tube; stigma pinhead.

J	F	M	A	M	J	J	A	S	O	N	D

Nick Helme

Erica lageniformis

Flask Heath

Stanford to Bredasdorp

FORM Upright shrublet to 50cm. **LEAVES** 3-whorled, needle-like, *minutely gland-toothed along the margins*. **FLOWERS** in clusters of up to 10 at the branch tips, on long stalks; bracteoles lance-shaped, near the base of the flower stalks. **SEPALS** lance-shaped. **COROLLA** vase-shaped and constricted at the throat, *21–33mm* long, hairless, sticky, white turning pink and with a dark throat; lobes spreading, pointed. **ANTHERS** 8, concealed, with a rough chin-like protuberance at the base and shortly awned. **STYLE** reaching the mouth of the tube; stigma pinhead.

J	F	M	A	M	J	J	A	S	O	N	D

Ross Turner

> Erica specialist E.G.H. 'Ted' Oliver includes *Erica shannonii* (formerly incorrectly spelled *Erica shannonea*) in this species.

Erica irbyana

Hawston to Elim

FORM Upright shrublet to 50cm.
LEAVES 3-whorled, needle-like, *minutely gland-toothed along the margins*.
FLOWERS in clusters of 3 to 8 at the branch tips, on long stalks; bracteoles lance-shaped, near the base of the flower stalks.
SEPALS lance-shaped. **COROLLA** vase-shaped and constricted at the throat, *12–20mm* long, hairless, sticky, pale to dark pink and with a dark throat; lobes spreading, ±pointed. **ANTHERS** 8, concealed, with a rough chin-like protuberance at the base and shortly awned. **STYLE** reaching the mouth of the tube; stigma pinhead.

This may be merely a small-flowered form of *Erica lageniformis* (opposite). Erica specialist E.G.H. 'Ted' Oliver considers it to be a subspecies of that species.

| J | F | M | A | M | J | J | A | S | O | N | D |

Erica curvifolia
Comb-leaved Heath

Seepages on slopes on the southwestern mountains from Jonkershoek and the Riviersonderend Mtns to the Hottentots Holland and Kleinrivier Mtns

FORM Upright, slender shrublet to 50cm, with ascending flowering branchlets. **LEAVES** 3-whorled, appressed to the stems, *almost scale-like, thick and leathery*, with *short, stout, gland-tipped bristles along the margins*, thus appearing finely toothed.

Erica specialist E.G.H. 'Ted' Oliver considers *Erica cristata* and *Erica trichroma* to be subspecies of *Erica curvifolia*.

FLOWERS in 3- to 6-flowered clusters or umbels at the tips of the branchlets, erect or suberect on stalks covered with gland-tipped bristles; bracteoles scale-like, with stout glands along the margins. **SEPALS** lance-shaped, with *stout glands along the margins in the upper part*. **COROLLA** tubular or urn-shaped, noticeably contracted around the mouth, *8–12mm* long, *velvety*, slightly sticky, pink to reddish with a purple ring around the top of the tube; lobes spreading, ±pointed. **ANTHERS** 8, concealed, with *slender tails at the base that are partially joined to the filaments*. **STYLE** concealed; stigma pinhead.

J	F	M	A	M	J	J	A	S	O	N	D

Nick Helme

Erica ventricosa
Wax Heath, Franschhoek Heath, Franschhoekheide

Franschhoek to Hottentots Holland Mtns

J	F	M	A	M	J	J	A	S	O	N	D

FORM Upright shrublet to 50cm or rarely up to 1m, often with additional flowering short-shoots in the upper leaf axils. **LEAVES** 4-whorled, widely spreading and *usually curved slightly upwards at the ends*, needle-like, *fringed with long, whisker-like hairs along the margins*. **FLOWERS** in dense clusters at the tips of the stems and of the short-shoots and then forming pyramidal masses, suberect or spreading on long stalks; bracteoles needle-like, fringed with hairs. **SEPALS** narrowly lance-shaped, *fringed with hairs*. **COROLLA** urn- or vase-

Nick Helme

shaped and narrowed to the mouth but not sharply constricted at the throat, 12–16mm long, hairless, glossy but not sticky, whitish or pale pink and with a darker throat; lobes spreading or curled back, ±pointed. **ANTHERS** 8, concealed, minutely crested at the base. **STYLE** reaching the mouth of the tube; stigma pinhead.

Erica coventryi

Seepages on mountain slopes, often forming dense stands, on the Kleinrivier Mtns

FORM Upright shrub to 1.2m, usually with a few additional flowering short-shoots in the upper leaf axils. **LEAVES** 4-whorled, needle-like and triangular in section. **FLOWERS** tightly clustered in 4s at the tips of the stems and on two or three additional short-shoots, aggregated into larger compound heads, suberect, *stalkless*; bracteoles needle-like with papery edges, fringed with whisker-like hairs and small glands. **SEPALS** needle-like, with *papery edges, almost as long as the corolla tube, fringed with long whisker-like bristles* mixed with stalked glands along the margins. **COROLLA** vase-shaped contracted like a drawstring to a very narrow mouth, 8–13mm long, ±hairless or minutely velvety on the tube, with a dark red tube and *lobes that are mealy white or pale pink above*; lobes spreading, elliptic-pointed. **ANTHERS** 8, concealed, rounded at the base. **STYLE** reaching the mouth of the tube; stigma concealed, reaching just below the mouth of the tube, pinhead.

These populations are sometimes considered to be a variety of *Erica fastigiata* (see p. 93).

(see p. 93)

| J | F | M | A | M | J | J | A | S | O | N | D |

Ross Turner

Ross Turner

Erica infundibuliformis

Funnelflower Heath

Cooler rocky slopes in seepages or boggy places and along streams from the eastern foothills of the Du Toitskloof Pass to Houwhoek

FORM Upright, willowy, slender-stemmed shrublet to 1.2m, stems bearing numerous flowering branchlets and closely congested short-shoots towards or below the ends. **LEAVES** 4-whorled, needle-like. **FLOWERS** mostly in 4s at the tips of the branches and short-shoots, aggregated in dense cylindrical or interrupted raceme-like plumes, suberect on short stalks or almost stalkless; bracteoles pressed against the calyx, needle-like. **SEPALS** needle-like and keeled, densely fringed with short hairs along the margins. **COROLLA** *narrowly cylindrical* and constricted at the top to a very narrow mouth, *16–20mm* long, hairless, *pale or deeper pink often flushed darker towards the top of the tube*, with white or pale pink lobes; lobes spreading, pointed. **ANTHERS** 8, concealed, rounded at the base. **STYLE** reaching just beyond the mouth of the tube; stigma pinhead.

This species was also known as *Erica pavettiflora*.

| J | F | M | A | M | J | J | A | S | O | N | D |

SIMILAR SPECIES *Erica lawsonii* from the Riviersonderend Mtns above Genadendal has the flowers strictly solitary at the tip of each short-shoot.

John Manning

Erica cylindrica

Moist slopes and along streams on the Elandskloof Mtns between Wolseley and Hermon
FORM Upright, willowy, slender-stemmed shrublet to 1.2m, often with vegetative shoots from the base, stems bearing numerous flowering branchlets and closely congested short-shoots towards or below the ends. **LEAVES** 4-whorled, needle-like. **FLOWERS** mostly in 4s at the tips of the branches and short-shoots, aggregated in dense cylindrical or interrupted raceme-like plumes, often with dead and fresh flowers together, suberect on short stalks, *sweetly clove-scented*; bracteoles pressed against the calyx, needle-like. **SEPALS** needle-like and fringed with short hairs along the margins. **COROLLA** *narrowly cylindrical* and constricted at the top to a very narrow mouth, *10–14mm* long, hairless, *creamy white to pale yellow*; lobes spreading, pointed. **ANTHERS** 8, concealed, rounded at the base. **STYLE** reaching just beyond the mouth of the tube; stigma pinhead.

The fragrant flowers are pollinated by large, hovering hawkmoths. Occasional pink-flowered hybrids with *Erica daphniflora* (see p. 94) have been recorded.

| J | F | M | A | M | J | J | A | S | O | N | D |

John Manning

Cluster 3 ■ SMALL VASE HEATHS

Smaller-flowered species with a hairless corolla up to 10mm long, tapering smoothly to the small mouth and with lance-shaped or needle-like sepals

Erica inflata

Inflated Heath

Sandy flats and plateaus or along streams in the western mountains from the Cederberg and Piketberg to Ceres

FORM Upright shrublet to 1m. **LEAVES** closely overlapping and 4-whorled or scattered, needle-like, *often long and slender, and bearing a slender awn at the tip.* **FLOWERS** several to many in a *leafless crowded raceme or cluster at the tip of the stem*, nodding on slender stalks; bracteoles needle-like, drawn into a slender awn at the tip, reddish. **SEPALS** needle-like, *drawn into a slender awn at the tip*, with *stalked glands along the margins*, reddish. **COROLLA** urn-shaped and constricted to a small mouth, *6–8mm* long, hairless and matte, pale to dark pink and often darker around the neck; lobes small, spreading, blunt. **ANTHERS** 8, concealed, with *long tails at the base.* **STYLE** concealed; stigma pinhead.

SIMILAR SPECIES *Erica praecox* from Du Toitskloof to the Hottentots Holland Mtns has velvety or shortly hairy leaves and slightly larger flowers 8–10mm long, with anthers that are rounded at the base.

J	F	M	A	M	J	J	A	S	O	N	D

Erica fastigiata

Four Sisters Heath, Four-flowered Heath

Seepages on mountain slopes, often forming dense stands, from Franschhoek to the Kogelberg and onto the Riviersonderend Mtns

| J | F | M | A | M | J | J | A | S | O | N | D |

FORM Upright shrub to 1.2m, often with additional flowering short-shoots along the stems. **LEAVES** 4-whorled, needle-like and triangular in section. **FLOWERS** tightly clustered in 4s at the tips of the branches and short-shoots, sometimes aggregated in dense head-like or interrupted raceme-like plumes, suberect, stalkless; bracteoles needle-like with papery edges. **SEPALS** needle-like with *papery edges, almost as long as the corolla tube*. **COROLLA** urn- or vase-shaped with a very narrow mouth, *5–10mm* long, hairless or minutely velvety on the neck, with the *tube flushed dark red* and *lobes that are mealy white above with dark green or red chevrons around the mouth*; lobes spreading, elliptic-pointed. **ANTHERS** 8, concealed, *rounded at the base*. **STYLE** reaching the mouth of the tube; stigma concealed, reaching just below the mouth of the tube, pinhead.

John Manning

Carina Lochner

Erica daphniflora

Daphne-flowered Heath

Mainly in seepages and along streams but also on damp rocky slopes from the Cederberg to the Du Toitskloof Mtns and inland along the western Langeberg to Swellendam

FORM Upright, willowy or sprawling, slender-stemmed shrublet to 1m, stems bearing numerous flowering branchlets and closely congested short-shoots towards or below the ends. **LEAVES** 4-whorled, needle-like. **FLOWERS** tightly clustered in 4s at the tips of the branches and short-shoots, aggregated in dense cylindrical or interrupted raceme-like clusters, suberect, stalkless, sweetly scented like honeysuckle; *bracteoles pressed against the calyx*, needle-like. **SEPALS** *lance-shaped* and *membranous towards the base* but *narrowed* and *needle-like* at the end. **COROLLA** vase-shaped with a *very narrow mouth, 6–8mm long*, hairless, white, yellow, green, red, orange, pink or bicoloured white and pink; lobes broad and spreading or curled back, pointed. **ANTHERS** 8, concealed, *rounded or pointed at the base*. **STYLE** concealed; stigma pinhead.

Distinguished from *Erica denticulata* (see p. 97) by having sepals that are not evidently toothed on the margins. Hybrids between the two species are known where they co-occur in the Groot Winterhoek Mtns above Porterville.

J	F	M	A	M	J	J	A	S	O	N	D

Nick Helme

Ismail Ebrahim

John Manning

John Manning

Ismail Ebrahim

John Manning

Colin Paterson-Jones

John Manning

Erica transparens

Cool, south-facing rocky slopes on the Cape Peninsula and Du Toitskloof Mtns eastwards along the coastal ranges to Uniondale and inland on the Swartberg and Kammanassie Mtns

FORM Erect, multi-stemmed shrublet to 40cm, *resprouting from a woody base*, stems bearing numerous flowering short-shoots. **LEAVES** 4-whorled, finely needle-like and triangular in section. **FLOWERS** tightly clustered in 4s at the tips of the branches and short-shoots, sometimes aggregated in dense head-like or interrupted raceme-like clusters, suberect, stalkless; *bracteoles pressed against the calyx*, scale-like and papery with bristles along the margins. **SEPALS** *lance-shaped* and *papery* with *bristles along the margins*. **COROLLA** vase-shaped with a very narrow mouth, *4–5mm* long, hairless, mostly pink but also white or red; lobes spreading, pointed. **ANTHERS** 8, concealed, *pointed at the base*. **STYLE** reaching the mouth of the tube; stigma concealed, pinhead.

J	F	M	A	M	J	J	A	S	O	N	D

Ross Turner

Nick Helme

Erica walkeri

Walker's Heath

Du Toitskloof Mtns

Like **Erica daphniflora** (see p. 94) but the **sepals are elliptical** with **finely jagged margins**, and the **flowers** are **pale pink** with **white lobes**; some forms are strongly honey-scented.

> This species was formerly incorrectly spelled *Erica walkeria*.

J	F	M	A	M	J	J	A	S	O	N	D

Nick Helme

Nick Helme

Erica denticulata

Sweet-scented Heath, Lekkerruikheide

Sandy flats to rocky upper slopes from Piketberg and Koue Bokkeveld to the Stellenbosch and Riviersonderend Mtns

FORM Upright or sprawling, slender-stemmed shrublet to 50cm, stems bearing numerous flowering branchlets and with short-shoots towards the ends. **LEAVES** 4-whorled, needle-like. **FLOWERS** tightly clustered in 4s at the tips of the branches and short-shoots, aggregated in dense head-like or interrupted raceme-like clusters, suberect, stalkless, scented like carnations; **bracteoles pressed against the calyx**, needle-like with ragged papery edges. **SEPALS elliptical** with a **needle-like tip** and **broad papery edges** that are **conspicuously jagged-toothed or torn**. **COROLLA** vase-shaped with a very narrow mouth, **6–8mm** long, hard and waxy, hairless, white, cream-coloured, greenish white, pale yellowish or pink; lobes broad and spreading or curled back, pointed. **ANTHERS** 8, concealed, **rounded at the base**. **STYLE** concealed; stigma pinhead.

John Manning

> Very like *Erica daphniflora* (see p. 94) but distinguished by the elliptical sepals with markedly jagged-toothed edges. Hybrids between the two species are known where the two species co-occur in the Groot Winterhoek Mtns above Porterville.

J	F	M	A	M	J	J	A	S	O	N	D

Cluster 4 ■ CHAFFY VASE HEATHS
Smaller-flowered species with a hairless corolla up to 10mm long, tapering smoothly to the small mouth and glossy, ±petal-like sepals

Erica albens

Pale Heath

Moist upper slopes of the Langeberg and Outeniqua Mtns and inland on the Swartberg

FORM Upright, willowy shrub to 1m. **LEAVES** 3-whorled, needle-like and triangular in section. **FLOWERS** solitary in upper leaf axils forming a dense, short or long raceme near the tops of the stems, suberect to nodding on stalks; bracteoles scale-like. **SEPALS** lance-shaped or almost petal-like, papery. **COROLLA** vase-shaped with a very narrow mouth, 6mm long, hairless, white or yellowish or pink-tinged; lobes spreading, pointed. **ANTHERS** 8, concealed, *minutely spurred at the base*. **STYLE** just reaching the mouth of the tube; stigma inconspicuous.

J	F	M	A	M	J	J	A	S	O	N	D

Rendert Hoekstra

Nick Helme

Erica lutea

Saffron-rice Heath, Geelrysheide

Moist upper slopes from the Cape Peninsula and Paarl to the Riviersonderend and Kleinrivier Mtns

> The almost papery flowers make a rustling sound when brushed.

FORM Upright, willowy shrub to 1m, with numerous slender flowering branches and branchlets. **LEAVES** *opposite in alternating pairs*, pressed against the branches, needle-like. **FLOWERS** mostly 1 or 2 (up to 4) on reduced scaly spurs in the uppermost leaf axils, arranged in small clusters or dense cylindrical false-racemes at the tops of the stems, on short stalks; bracteoles scale-like. **SEPALS** broad and suborbicular with a short point, ±half as long as the corolla tube, *widely overlapping in two pairs* with the *inner pair slightly larger*, papery, petal-like and coloured like the corolla. **COROLLA** vase-shaped with a very narrow mouth, nodding, *7–10mm long*, hairless, white or yellow; lobes small and spreading, pointed. **ANTHERS** 8, concealed, with crested tails at the base. **STYLE** concealed; stigma pinhead.

J	F	M	A	M	J	J	A	S	O	N	D

Ross Turner

John Manning

Erica tenuifolia

Fine-leaved Heath

Cape Peninsula and Paarl to the Riviersonderend Mtns

FORM Upright, willowy shrublet to 60cm, with slender flowering branches and branchlets. **LEAVES** *opposite in alternating pairs or* the *upper ones 3-whorled*, pressed against the branches, needle-like. **FLOWERS** 1 to 3 on reduced scaly spurs in the uppermost leaf axils, arranged in small clusters at the tops of the stems, on short stalks; bracteoles scale-like. **SEPALS** broad and suborbicular with a short point, more than half as long as to ±as long as the corolla tube, *widely overlapping in two pairs*, with the *inner pair slightly larger*, papery, petal-like and coloured like the corolla. **COROLLA** vase-shaped with a very narrow mouth, nodding, *5–6mm* long, hairless, pale to deep pink; lobes small and spreading, pointed. **ANTHERS** 8, concealed, with crested tails at the base. **STYLE** concealed; stigma pinhead.

This may just be a form of *Erica lutea* (see p. 99) with smaller, pink flowers.

J F M A M J J A S O N D

SIMILAR SPECIES Erica steinbergiana from the Outeniqua and Tsitsikamma Mtns has similar flowers but the anthers are rounded at the base, and the plants have numerous short flowering branchlets arising successively up the stems, so that the flowerheads form a dense plume up the length of the stem; **Erica bracteolaris** from the Langeberg Mtns between Swellendam and Heidelberg has slightly larger flowers, with the corolla 7–10mm long and paddle-shaped sepals that are narrowed at the base but widened above, with a short point and ±as long as the corolla tube, and anthers that are rounded at the base.

Nick Helme

Erica taxifolia

Yew-leaved Heath

Groot Winterhoek Mtns above Tulbagh to the Riviersonderend Mtns

FORM Upright, wand-like shrublet to 60cm, usually with short flowering branchlets arising successively up the stems. **LEAVES** 3-whorled, rather large and awl-like. **FLOWERS** in head-like clusters at the tips of the branches, stalked; bracteoles lance-shaped, dry and papery, ±pressed against the calyx. **SEPALS** large and leaf-shaped, ±as long as the corolla tube, overlapping in two pairs, papery, petal-like and coloured like the corolla. **COROLLA** vase-shaped with a very narrow mouth, erect, *6–9mm* long, hairless, bright pink with mostly darker lobes; lobes small and ±spreading, pointed. **ANTHERS** 8, concealed, *spurred or shortly tailed at the base*. **STYLE** concealed; stigma pinhead.

J	F	M	A	M	J	J	A	S	O	N	D

Carina Lochner

Erica corifolia

Leathery-leaved Heath, Dark-tip Heath

Sandy flats and mountain slopes from the Cape Peninsula to De Hoop

FORM Upright, wand-like or willowy shrublet to 1m, sometimes with short flowering branchlets arising successively up the stems so that the flowerheads form short false-racemes. **LEAVES** 3-whorled, suberect or pressed against the stem, needle-like or awl-like. **FLOWERS** 1 to 3 on reduced spur-shoots at the tips of the branchlets, forming a cluster at the tops of the stems and sometimes also on short-shoots near the tops of the stems, stalked; bracteoles lance-shaped, dry and papery, pink. **SEPALS** large and leaf-shaped, more than half as long as or longer than the corolla tube, overlapping in two pairs, papery, petal-like and coloured like the corolla, with darker tips. **COROLLA** vase-shaped with a very narrow mouth, erect, *3–6mm* long, hairless, bright pink to reddish; lobes small and ±spreading, pointed. **ANTHERS** 8, concealed, with *jagged crests at the base*. **STYLE** reaching mouth of tube; stigma pinhead.

Nick Helme

> This species was formerly spelled *Erica coriifolia*.

J	F	M	A	M	J	J	A	S	O	N	D

GROOP 2 VASE HEATHS ▨ **Cluster 4** CHAFFY VASE HEATHS ▨ **101**

Erica rhopalantha

Club-flowered Heath

Kogelberg to Bredasdorp

FORM Upright, *rounded or compact shrublet* to 50cm, sometimes with short flowering branchlets arising successively up the stems so that the flowerheads form short false-racemes. **LEAVES** 3-whorled, pressed against the stem, needle-like or awl-like. **FLOWERS** 1 to 3 on reduced spur-shoots at the tips of the branchlets, forming a cluster at the tops of the stems and often also on short-shoots near the tops of the stems, aggregated into interrupted false-racemes, stalked; bracteoles scale-like, dry and papery, pink. **SEPALS** large and leaf-shaped, more than half as long as or longer than the corolla tube, overlapping in two pairs, papery, petal-like and coloured like the corolla, with darker tips. **COROLLA** broadly vase-shaped with a very narrow mouth, nodding, *3–4mm long*, hairless, *dark purplish pink*; lobes small and ±spreading, pointed. **ANTHERS** 8, concealed, with *jagged crests at the base*. **STYLE** reaching mouth of tube; stigma pinhead.

| J | F | M | A | M | J | J | A | S | O | N | D |

Jenny Parsons

Colin Paterson-Jones

Warren McLelland

GROUP 3
SMALL-FLOWER HEATHS

Smaller-flowered species with an urn- or goblet-shaped corolla 3–10mm long, with 8 anthers

Cluster 1 ■ SMALL BOTTLEBRUSH HEATHS
Flowers 1 or 2 in the axils of the upper leaves, arranged in a dense cylindrical raceme or spike towards the tops of the stems

Erica empetrina
Crowberry Heath

Marshy places on the summit plateau of Table Mountain on the Cape Peninsula
FORM Upright shrublet to 60cm, with closely leafy flowering stems.
LEAVES *6-whorled*, the lower leaves spreading but the upper leaves erect and closely overlapping, needle-like, *with short bristles* on the lower surface and along the margins. **FLOWERS** solitary in the upper leaf axils forming a dense cylindrical head or spike at or near the tips of the stems, *spreading on short stalks* or *almost stalkless*; bracteoles scale-like. **SEPALS** lance-shaped, fringed with bristles along the margins and towards the tip. **COROLLA** urn-shaped, 4–5mm long, hairless or hairy, *pink to dark red*; lobes erect, rounded. **ANTHERS** 8, partially protruding, with *crests at the base*. **OVARY** velvety. **STYLE** protruding beyond the anthers; stigma pinhead.

This species was formerly incorrectly known under the name *Erica empetrifolia*.

| J | F | M | A | M | J | J | A | S | O | N | D |

Corinne Merry

Corinne Merry

Erica pyxidiflora

Bottlebrush Heath

Marshy places on mountains of the Cape Peninsula from Table Mountain to Smitswinkel Bay

Very similar to **Erica empetrina** but with **cream-coloured flowers tinged pink**, a **short bristly chin** at the base of the anthers, and a **hairless ovary**.

| J | F | M | A | M | J | J | A | S | O | N | D |

Ross Turner

Corinne Merry

Erica viscaria subsp. viscaria

Sticky Heath, Klokkiesheide

Flats and lower slopes on the Cape Peninsula and adjacent flats between Malmesbury and Eersterivier

Includes forms previously known as *Erica decora*. See p. 58 for a complete description of this species, including the larger-flowered subspecies.

| J | F | M | A | M | J | J | A | S | O | N | D |

FORM Upright shrub to 1m. **LEAVES** *4- or 6-whorled*, needle-like, finely velvety on both surfaces. **FLOWERS** solitary in the upper leaf axils in a short, dense raceme near the tops of the stems, suberect on short stalks; bracteoles needle-like. **SEPALS** needle-like or more rarely lance-shaped, minutely velvety. **COROLLA** tubular and very slightly constricted at the mouth, *8-ribbed longitudinally, slightly curved*, 5–9mm long, *minutely bristly, slightly sticky*, purplish pink; lobes slightly spreading, blunt. **ANTHERS** 8, deeply concealed, *rounded or toothed at the base*. **OVARY** covered with long white hairs. **STYLE** concealed or reaching just beyond the mouth of the corolla; stigma pinhead.

Nick Helme

Erica pulchella

Sandy flats and slope from the Cape Peninsula along the coastal plain to Albertinia
FORM Upright shrublet to 60cm, with numerous ascending branches and branchlets.
LEAVES 3-whorled, erect and pressed against the stems, needle-like. **FLOWERS** solitary
in the upper leaf axils forming a dense cylindrical raceme near the tips of the stems,
nodding on short stalks; bracteoles needle-like. **SEPALS** large and lance-shaped or almost
petal-like but leathery, the *margins densely fringed with backward-pointing hairs*.
COROLLA shortly tubular or bell-shaped, 4mm long, hairless, pink to dark red (rarely white);
lobes slightly spreading above, rounded. **ANTHERS** 8, concealed, with *long horns* at the
base that are *partly joined to the filaments*. **STYLE** concealed; stigma pinhead.

Includes forms previously known
as *Erica longiaristata*.

| J | F | M | A | M | J | J | A | S | O | N | D |

Nick Helme

Ross Turner

John Manning

Erica parilis

Yellowspike Heath

Dry stony slopes from the Cederberg along the western mountains to Du Toitskloof
FORM Stiffly upright shrublet to 1(–2)m, with ascending branches. **LEAVES** 3-, 4- or 6-
whorled, erect and curved inwards, needle-like or almost leaf-shaped, 3-angled, minutely
velvety on the upper surface. **FLOWERS** solitary in the upper leaf axils forming a dense
conical or cylindrical raceme near the tips of the stems, nodding on stalks; bracteoles
needle-like. **SEPALS** *needle-like, sometimes almost as long as the corolla, yellow*.
COROLLA tubular or narrowly bell-shaped, 4–10mm long, hairless or velvety, dry or
slightly sticky, *bright yellow*; lobes spreading above, rounded. **ANTHERS** 8, partly or
fully protruding, with short spurs at the base that are partly joined to the filaments.
STYLE protruding; stigma clearly knob-like.

| J | F | M | A | M | J | J | A | S | O | N | D |

SIMILAR SPECIES *Erica campanularis*
from the Hottentots Holland to the Kleinrivier
Mtns has fewer bell-shaped yellow flowers,
7mm long, with the anthers at the very
bottom of the cup clasping the ovary.

Erica pannosa

Damp slopes on the Riviersonderend Mtns; very common around Greyton

| J | F | M | A | M | J | J | A | S | O | N | D |

FORM Erect or somewhat straggling shrublet to 1m, with numerous short, ascending flowering shoots, the *branches covered in a mix of short, velvety hairs and long, gland-tipped hairs*. **LEAVES** rather *loosely scattered lower on the stems but loosely 4-whorled above*, leaf-like and spreading with the margins scarcely rolled over at the very edges to leave the *underside mostly exposed, very sticky*, covered with a mix of short, velvety hairs and whisker-like gland-tipped hairs. **FLOWERS** in nodding clusters or umbels at the tips of the branches and branchlets, on short or longer whitish stalks covered in a mix of felted and slender gland-tipped hairs; bracteoles solitary, scale-like or spoon-shaped with a slender stalk, covered with long sticky hairs. **SEPALS** lance-shaped, covered with a mix of *felted hairs and long, whisker-like, gland-tipped hairs*, white with green tips. **COROLLA** urn-shaped, 5mm long, *velvety or felted with backward-facing hairs*, white, soon turning brown; lobes erect, short and blunt. **ANTHERS** 8, concealed, *crested at the base*. **STYLE** reaching just beyond the mouth of the tube; stigma pinhead.

John Manning

SIMILAR SPECIES *Erica perlata* from the same localities has slightly smaller, cup-shaped flowers, 3–4mm long, with a more open mouth exposing the anthers, which are rounded or minutely horned at the base.

John Manning

Erica caffra

Water Heath

Streamsides and wet slopes from near Nieuwoudtville to the Cape Peninsula eastwards along the coastal ranges and inland on the Swartberg to KwaZulu-Natal

FORM Upright, rather *stiff shrub or small tree, 2–4m*, with numerous ascending, *pale grey flowering branchlets*. **LEAVES** 3-whorled, narrow and loosely spreading, with the *margins rolled over only at the very edges* to leave wide *pale grey strips either side of the underside midvein*. **FLOWERS** solitary in the upper leaf axils of the branches and branchlets in short clusters or interrupted false-racemes, aggregated into narrow panicles, suberect on stalks, honey-scented; bracteoles scale-like, silky. **SEPALS** lance-shaped, *silky*. **COROLLA** urn-shaped with a narrow mouth, 5–6mm long, *velvety, white or yellowish*; lobes spreading, short and blunt. **ANTHERS** 8, concealed, horned at the base. **STYLE** just reaching the mouth of the tube; stigma pinhead.

J | F | M | A | M | J | J | A | S | O | N | D

John Manning

Ross Turner

Sarlie Gouws

Erica irregularis

Gansbaai Heath, Gansbaaiheide

Coastal flats and hills in deep, neutral-pH sands from Stanford to Gansbaai

FORM Upright shrublet to 1.5cm, with erect flowering branches. **LEAVES** 3- or 4-whorled, needle-like, triangular in cross-section. **FLOWERS** solitary in each axil on individual scaly stubs and often also in a small tuft at the tips of the branches, forming a dense, plume-like raceme towards the ends of the branches, nodding on *white-felted stalks covered with branched hairs*; bracts and bracteoles scale-like. **SEPALS** leaf-shaped, *strongly keeled, glossy* and *papery, slightly more than half as long as the corolla* and coloured like it. **COROLLA** urn-shaped with a small mouth, 4–5mm long, hairless, pale or deeper shell-pink; lobes erect, rounded. **ANTHERS** 8, concealed, *crested at the base*. **STYLE** concealed; stigma pinhead.

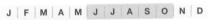

J | F | M | A | M | J | J | A | S | O | N | D

Erica rubiginosa

Clay banks and gravelly flats from Bot River to Agulhas

J | F | M | A | M | J | J | A | S | O | N | D

Petra Broddle

FORM Upright shrublet to 30cm, with erect flowering branches, the lower leaves bearing the dry, knob-like remains of the flower stalks in their axils. **LEAVES** 3-whorled, needle-like. **FLOWERS** 1 to 3 in the upper leaf axils on individual scaly stubs, forming a dense raceme towards the ends of the branches, nodding on *slender, hairless white stalks*; bracts and bracteoles scale-like, white. **SEPALS** leaf-shaped, *strongly keeled, almost as long as the corolla* and coloured like it. **COROLLA** cup-shaped, *2–3mm* long, hairless, white or pale pink; lobes erect or spreading above, rounded. **ANTHERS** 8, *almost fully protruding, tapered towards the base.* **STYLE** protruding beyond anthers and *curved upwards*; stigma pinhead.

Erica nudiflora

Widely distributed on granite and sandstone flats and slopes from the Cederberg and the Witteberg to the Cape Peninsula and eastwards to Bredasdorp

FORM Upright, compact or sprawling shrublet to 50cm, with erect flowering branches, sometimes with additional flowering branchlets developing in the upper part.

J | F | M | A | M | J | J | A | S | O | N | D

LEAVES 3-whorled, needle-like, *with whisker-like hairs* or *bristles along the margins* and often also the underside. **FLOWERS** 1 or 2 on *thread-like stalks* in the upper leaf axils in loose, cylindrical racemes or aggregated into panicles, nodding; bracteoles near the base of the flower stalks, scale-like, bristly along the margins. **SEPALS** needle-like, *bristly along the edges*. **COROLLA** narrowly urn-shaped, 4-ribbed and 4-angled at the base, 3–5mm long, hairless, pink; lobes erect, small, rounded. **ANTHERS** 8, *fully protruding*, rather loosely arranged, *covered with spinules, rounded at the base*. **STYLE** protruding beyond the anthers; stigma pinhead.

Nick Helme

Erica scytophylla

Locally common from Bredasdorp to De Hoop

FORM Upright shrublet to 1m, with erect flowering branches, sometimes with more flowering branchlets developing in the upper part. **LEAVES** 3-whorled, needle-like or almost scale-like, *thick*. **FLOWERS** solitary on *long, thread-like stalks* from a scaly stub in the upper leaf axils, in dense, rounded or cylindrical racemes, nodding, *stalks reddish* and *covered with short, backward-facing hairs*; bracteoles towards the middle of the flower stalk, scale-like, **SEPALS** scale-like, reddish. **COROLLA** urn-shaped, 4-ribbed and 4-angled at the base, 3–5mm long, hairless, pink or sometimes white flushing pink when drying; lobes erect, small, rounded. **ANTHERS** 8, *fully protruding*, rather loosely arranged, *covered with spinules*, with *short spurs at the base*. **STYLE** protruding beyond the anthers; stigma pinhead.

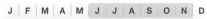

| J | F | M | A | M | J | J | A | S | O | N | D |

Cluster 2 ■ GOBLET HEATHS
Corolla cup- or goblet-shaped, with a short tube 1–4mm long
and large cupped-lobes that are as long as or longer than the tube

Erica leucanthera

Pale Heath

Seeps and cool slopes on western mountains from the Cederberg to Franschhoek and onto the Riviersonderend Mtns

This is the only erica with pale yellow anthers.

FORM Upright shrublet to 90cm, with numerous erect flowering branchlets arising successively up the stems to form long plumes, the branchlets felted with plumose hairs. **LEAVES** 3-whorled, spreading or pressed against the stem, scale-like or shortly needle-like, yellowish green. **FLOWERS** mostly in 3s at the tips of the short-shoots aggregated into dense, plume-like panicles, spreading or suberect on short stalks, sweetly fruit-scented; bracteoles scale-like, papery and coloured like the corolla. **SEPALS** petal-like and papery, overlapping in two opposite pairs, keeled above, more than half as long as the corolla and coloured like it. **COROLLA** cup-shaped, 4-angled between the sepals, 2–3mm long with a very shallow tube 1mm long and as long as or shorter than the lobes, hairless, *pale yellow or creamy white*; lobes spreading above, cupped, rounded. **ANTHERS** 8, *pale yellow*, initially arranged spoke-like around the style but soon loosely spreading, protruding beyond the tube and either held within the corolla cup or just protruding beyond the tips of the lobes, *V-shaped with splayed lobes, rounded at the base*. **STYLE** protruding beyond anthers; stigma pinhead.

J | F | M | A | M | J | J | A | S | O | N | D

Erica sparsa

Floriferous Heath

Common on sandy flats and lower slopes in the southern coastal regions from George to Humansdorp and the Cockscomb Mtns

> This species was previously (and more appropriately) known as *Erica floribunda*.

FORM Upright shrublet to 90cm, with numerous ascending branchlets and short-shoots, the **branchlets felted with plumose hairs**. **LEAVES** 3-whorled, needle-like. **FLOWERS** mostly in 3s along the branchlets, forming false-racemes aggregated into dense panicles, nodding on short stalks; bracteoles scale-like, papery and coloured like the corolla. **SEPALS** petal-like and papery, coloured like the corolla and ±half as long. **COROLLA** cup-shaped, 1–2mm long with a very shallow tube 0.5–0.75mm long that is shorter than the lobes, hairless, white to pale pink; lobes erect, cupped, rounded. **ANTHERS** 8, protruding from the tube but held within the corolla cup, **rounded at the base**. **STYLE** **protruding far beyond anthers**; stigma widened and **cup-shaped, reddish**.

Nicky van Berkel

J F M A M J J A S O N D

Erica peltata

Shield-stigma Heath, Raasheide

Southwestern and southern coastal regions from the Riviersonderend Mtns along the Langeberg and Outeniqua Mtns to George

Easily confused with **Erica sparsa**, the two species sometimes even growing together, but distinguished by its often **slightly shorter style** and **broader, saucer-shaped stigma**.

J F M A M J J A S O N D

Nick Helme

Erica macrotrema

Dry, stony and rocky places, and common along the interior mountains from the Koue Bokkeveld and Swartruggens to the Witteberg

The plants produce clouds of pollen when disturbed.

J | F | M | A | M | J | J | A | **S** | **O** | **N** | D

John Manning

FORM Upright shrub to 1.5(–2)m, with numerous ascending branchlets and short-shoots, the branchlets felted with backward-facing simple and plumose hairs. **LEAVES** 3-whorled, scale-like, pressed against the branches, minutely velvety on the upper surface and with large glands along the margins. **FLOWERS** mostly in 3s on scaly spurs along the branchlets, forming false-racemes aggregated into dense panicles, nodding on short velvety stalks; ***bracts and bracteoles pressed against the sepals***, scale-like, papery and coloured like the corolla. **SEPALS** lance-shaped and almost petal-like, papery, coloured like the corolla and ±half as long.

COROLLA cup-shaped, 2mm long with a shallow tube 1mm long that is as long as the lobes, hairless, pink to brownish red or purple; lobes erect, cupped, rounded. **ANTHERS** 8, protruding from the tube but held within the corolla cup, with a ***large pore*** two-thirds the length of the lobes, ***minutely bristly, rounded at the base***. **STYLE** protruding far beyond anthers; stigma ***widened*** and ***cup-shaped***, reddish.

Erica seriphiifolia

Rocky slopes in seepages or in cool, moist places on Rooiberg near Calitzdorp in the Little Karoo and along the southern coastal mountains from Swellendam to Uniondale

FORM Erect shrublet to 40cm, with numerous flowering branchlets bearing short-shoots near the tips. **LEAVES** ***4-whorled, erect-incurved***, needle-like, mostly ***less than 4mm*** long.

FLOWERS 1 to 3 at the tips of the branchlets, and the short-shoots clustered into a round head at the tips of the branchlets, nodding on ***stalks covered with plumed or branched hairs; bracteoles narrow*** and ***spoon-shaped***, papery, pink. **SEPALS** large, papery and petal-like, rather loosely spreading and cupped, keeled near the tip, pink. **COROLLA** cup-shaped, 3–4mm long, hairless, deep pink; lobes large and cupped, ±pointed. **ANTHERS** 8, fully protruding from the tube but included in the cup, rounded at the base but pointed at the tips with a bristly peak. **STYLE** protruding; stigma pinhead.

J | F | M | A | M | J | J | A | **S** | **O** | **N** | **D**

Nicky van Berkel

Erica cubica

Box Heath

Seeps, marshes and along streams on lower southern slopes of the southern coastal mountains from Swellendam to KwaZulu-Natal

FORM Erect shrublet to 45cm, with numerous flowering branchlets bearing short-shoots near the tips. **LEAVES** *4-whorled or closely and irregularly packed, erect-incurved to spreading-incurved*, needle-like, *mostly more than 5mm long*. **FLOWERS** 1 to 3 at the tips of the branchlets and the short-shoots clustered into a round head at the tips of the branchlets, nodding on *stalks covered with plumed or branched hairs; bracteoles narrow* and *spoon-shaped*, papery, pink. **SEPALS** large, papery and petal-like, rather loosely spreading and cupped, keeled near the tip, pink. **COROLLA** goblet-shaped, with a rather box-shaped tube, 4–6mm long, hairless, deep pink; lobes large and cupped, ±pointed. **ANTHERS** 8, fully protruding from the tube but included in the cup, rounded at the base but pointed at the tips with a bristly peak. **STYLE** protruding; stigma pinhead.

| J | F | M | A | M | J | J | A | S | O | N | D |

Erica humifusa

Restricted to rock sheets on western and inland mountains from the Cederberg to the Hex River and Riviersonderend Mtns, and eastwards along the Swartberg to Kouga Mtns

FORM Erect, compact or sprawling shrublet to 20cm, with numerous flowering branchlets and short-shoots near the ends of the branches. **LEAVES** 3-whorled, *pressed against the stems, scale-like*. **FLOWERS** in 3s at the tips of the branchlets and short-shoots, arranged in interrupted false-racemes, nodding on *hairless, reddish stalks*; bracteoles papery and scale-like or lance-shaped, rather loosely spreading, pink. **SEPALS** large, papery and petal-like, relatively loosely spreading and cupped, keeled near the tip, pink. **COROLLA** goblet-shaped, narrowed below the mouth then widened, *2–4mm* long, hairless, pale to rosy pink; lobes large and cupped, ±pointed. **ANTHERS** 8, fully protruding from the tube but included in the cup, rounded at the base but pointed at the tips with a peak. **STYLE** protruding; stigma pinhead or disc-like.

| J | F | M | A | M | J | J | A | S | O | N | D |

John Manning

Erica cristiflora

Rocky slopes, usually in cooler or moist places on western mountain ranges from the Cederberg to the Cape Peninsula

FORM Erect, densely branched shrublet to 60cm, with numerous flowering branchlets and short-shoots near the ends of the branches. **LEAVES** 3-whorled, needle-like. **FLOWERS** 3 or more at the tips of the branchlets and short-shoots, arranged in interrupted false-racemes and narrow panicles, on *stalks covered with straight, velvety hairs*, sometimes with a musky or vanilla-like scent; bracteoles papery and petal-like, rather loosely spreading, pink. **SEPALS** large, papery and petal-like, rather loosely spreading and cupped, keeled near the tip, pink. **COROLLA** goblet-shaped, narrowed below the mouth then widened, *2–4mm* long, hairless, pale to rosy pink; lobes large and cupped, ±pointed. **ANTHERS** 8, fully protruding from the tube but included in the cup, rounded at the base but pointed at the tips with a bristly peak or crest. **STYLE** protruding; stigma pinhead or disc-like.

J F M A M J J A S O N D

Nick Helme

John Manning

John Manning

Erica melanthera
Black-anther Heath

Moist lower and upper slopes along the southern coastal and inland mountains from Ashton to Kariega and inland on the Swartberg and adjacent mountains in the Little Karoo

J	F	M	A	M	J	J	A	S	O	N	D

FORM Erect or somewhat spreading shrublet to 60cm, with numerous flowering branchlets arising successively up the stems so that the flowerheads form a plume up the length of the stems. **LEAVES** 3-whorled, needle-like, covered with short bristles mixed with scattered gland-tipped hairs or hairless. **FLOWERS** in 3s on the short-shoots, arranged in plume-like false-racemes towards the ends of the branches, aggregated into panicles, stalked; bracteoles lance-shaped, dry and papery, hairless or velvety. **SEPALS** *joined in the lower half into a cup-shaped calyx*, the *lobes ±as long as the corolla tube*, broader than long and keeled, overlapping in two pairs, petal-like and coloured like the corolla, *velvety or hairless.* **COROLLA** cup-shaped with a short tube, spreading or slightly nodding, 3–5mm long, hairless, pale to dark pink; lobes large and cupped, blunt. **ANTHERS** 8, completely protruding but held within the cupped lobes, black, rounded at the base but pointed at the tip. **STYLE** protruding well beyond the anthers; stigma pinhead.

Erica canaliculata
Channelled Heath

Moist flats and lower slopes of the Outeniqua and Tsitsikamma Mtns from George to Humansdorp

J	F	M	A	M	J	J	A	S	O	N	D

FORM Erect shrub to 2m or more, with numerous flowering branchlets arising successively up the stems so that the flowerheads form a plume up the length of the stems. **LEAVES** 3-whorled, needle-like, minutely hairy or hairless. **FLOWERS** in 3s on the short-shoots, arranged in plume-like false-racemes towards the ends of the branches, aggregated into panicles, stalked; bracteoles scale-like, minutely hairy. **SEPALS** *joined in the lower quarter into a shallow shaped calyx, lobes twice as long as the corolla tube*, ±as broad as long, almost petal-like and coloured like the corolla. **COROLLA** cup-shaped with a short tube, spreading or slightly nodding, 3–5mm long, hairless, pale to dark pink; lobes large and cupped, blunt. **ANTHERS** 8, completely protruding but held within the cupped lobes, black, rounded at the base but pointed at the tip. **STYLE** protruding well beyond the anthers; stigma pinhead.

Erica corydalis
White Petticoat Heath, Witrokheide

Moist upper southern slopes from the Houwhoek to Kleinrivier Mtns

FORM Upright or straggling, slender shrublet to 50cm, with erect branchlets with flowering spur-shoots in the upper axils. **LEAVES** 3-whorled, spreading, scale-like, glossy, pointed. **FLOWERS** 1 to 4 at the tips of highly reduced, scaly spur-shoots towards the ends of the branches, aggregated in loose or dense clusters or false-racemes, nodding on short stalks, strongly scented; bracteoles scale-like, hard and glossy. **SEPALS** large and petal-like, keeled, overlapping in two pairs, *hard and glossy*, with *large glands along the margins*, ±as long as the corolla tube, *white*. **COROLLA** *goblet-shaped* with a *swollen or globe-like tube constricted to a narrow mouth* with large cup-like lobes slightly longer than the tube, 4–5mm long, hairless, *white turning brown when bruised*; lobes cupped, rounded. **ANTHERS** 8, protruding from the tube but held within the corolla cup, *tailed or crested at the base*. **STYLE** protruding beyond the anthers; stigma pinhead.

| J | F | M | A | M | J | J | A | S | O | N | D |

Nick Helme

Erica thunbergii
Malay Heath, Yellow-petticoat Heath, Geelrokheide

Seasonally moist sandy flats and slopes from the Cederberg to the Koue Bokkeveld Mtns

FORM Upright, slender shrublet to 60cm, with erect branchlets bearing flowering spur-shoots in the upper axils. **LEAVES** 3-whorled, pressed against the branches, needle-like, microscopically hairy. **FLOWERS** solitary in the upper axils of the spur-shoots and often 3-whorled, aggregated in loose or dense clusters or interrupted false-racemes, nodding on long stalks; bracteoles leaf-shaped and keeled, papery, bright yellow and petal-like. **SEPALS** large and petal-like, keeled, overlapping in two pairs, *papery, rather loose*, ±as long as or longer than the corolla tube, *bright yellow*. **COROLLA** *goblet-shaped* with a *swollen or globe-like tube constricted to a narrow mouth* with large cup-like lobes slightly longer than the tube, *6–9mm* long, hairless, *bright scarlet with a whitish tube*; lobes cupped, pointed. **ANTHERS** 8, fully protruding from the tube but held within the corolla cup, *rounded or pointed at the base*. **STYLE** shortly protruding; stigma pinhead.

| J | F | M | A | M | J | J | A | S | O | N | D |

Colin Paterson-Jones

Sepals large, papery and petal-like, forming a colourful 'cloak' around the cup- or urn-shaped corolla; anthers mostly with jagged crests at the base

Erica calycina

Calycine Heath

Sandy flats and rocky slopes of the western mountains from the Cederberg to Riviersonderend and the Cape Peninsula

FORM Upright shrublet to 1(–2)m, the rod-like *stems felted with velvety and tufted hairs* and bearing numerous flowering branchlets arising successively up the stems, so that the flowers form plumes or narrow panicles up the length of the stems. **LEAVES** 3-whorled, needle-like, with *minute tufted hairs along the margins*. **FLOWERS** mostly in 3s at the tips of the flowering branchlets and short-shoots, arranged in plume-like racemes or narrow panicles towards the ends of the branches, nodding on *velvety stalks*; bracteoles near the top of the flower stalk just beneath the calyx, scale-like, papery, coloured like the corolla. **SEPALS** broadly leaf-shaped and overlapping in two opposite pairs, ±as long as the corolla tube, glossy and coloured like the corolla. **COROLLA** bell-shaped, 3–4mm long, hairless, sometimes slightly sticky, white or pale pink to purple; *lobes curved outwards, almost as long as the corolla tube*, blunt. **ANTHERS** 8, reaching just beyond and exposed in the open mouth of the tube, with large toothed crests at the base. **STYLE** protruding beyond the anthers; stigma pinhead.

| J | F | M | A | M | J | J | A | S | O | N | D |

John Manning

John Manning

Erica lucida

Along the western mountains from the Gifberg near Vanrhynsdorp through the Cederberg to the Hottentots Holland Mtns and Montagu

Like **Erica calycina** (opposite) and possibly not distinct from it, with **feather-like hairs on the stems**, and **pink to purple flowers** with **slightly shorter corolla lobes** ±half as long as the tube.

Erica triflora

Tri-flowered Heath

Du Toitskloof to the Hottentots Holland Mtns and Table Mountain

FORM Upright or sprawling shrublet or shrub to 3m, with erect stems and **flowering branchlets covered with barbed or plumed hairs**. **LEAVES** 3-whorled, needle-like. **FLOWERS** solitary in the upper axils of the flowering branches and often 4-whorled, nodding, stalked; bracteoles leaf-shaped and keeled, appressed against the sepals, papery, petal-like, white, sometimes with a red median streak. **SEPALS** large and petal-like, keeled, papery, rather loose, almost as long as the corolla, white or with a red streak. **COROLLA** broadly urn-shaped, **5–6mm** long, hairless, white; lobes small, erect, rounded. **ANTHERS** 8, concealed, with large toothed crests at the base. **STYLE** concealed, short and stout; stigma pinhead.

Erica tegulifolia

Tile-leaved Heath, Banketheide

Mainly drier, rocky eastern slopes from Du Toitskloof to the Hottentots Holland Mtns

FORM Upright shrub to 1m, with erect, closely leafy stems bearing numerous ascending flowering branchlets nodding at the tips. **LEAVES** 3-whorled, *closely overlapping* and *completely covering the stems, scale-like*. **FLOWERS** in 3s at the tips of the branchlets, nodding on short stalks; bracteoles leaf-shaped and keeled, loosely appressed against the sepals, papery, petal-like and coloured like the corolla. **SEPALS** large and petal-like, keeled, papery and transversely wrinkled, almost as long as the corolla and coloured like it. **COROLLA** urn-shaped, 4-angled at the base, *5–6mm* long, hairless, pale to deep pink; lobes erect and often almost closing the mouth, rather pointed. **ANTHERS** 8, concealed, with large toothed crests at the base. **STYLE** concealed, short and stout; stigma pinhead.

J | F | M | A | M | J | J | A | S | O | N | D

Nick Helme

Erica baccans

Berry Heath

Sandy flats and slopes on the Cape Peninsula

FORM Upright or sprawling shrublet or shrub to 3m, with erect, hairless stems and flowering branchlets. **LEAVES** *4-whorled*, needle-like, minutely toothed along the margins. **FLOWERS** solitary in the upper axils of the flowering branches and often 4-whorled, nodding, stalked; bracteoles leaf-shaped and keeled, papery, pale pink and petal-like. **SEPALS** large and petal-like, keeled, papery, rather loose, almost as long as the corolla, pale pink. **COROLLA** globe-shaped, with *4 indentations in the tube opposite the sepals* so that the *tube bulges between the sepals*, constricted to a narrow mouth, *5–6mm* long, hairless, pale pink with dark pink lobes; lobes small, erect, rounded. **ANTHERS** 8, concealed, with large toothed crests at the base. **STYLE** concealed, short and stout; stigma pinhead.

Nick Helme

J | F | M | A | M | J | J | A | S | O | N | D

Erica brevifolia

Seasonally moist mountain slopes or seepages on the Cape Peninsula and Hottentots Holland Mtns and eastwards along the Langeberg and Outeniqua Mtns to George

FORM Upright shrublet to 60cm, with mostly hairless stems and numerous erect flowering branchlets. **LEAVES** 3-whorled, *scale-like*. **FLOWERS** mostly in 3s at the tips of the flowering branchlets, nodding, stalked; bracteoles leaf-shaped, pale pink and petal-like. **SEPALS** large and petal-like, keeled, papery, rather loose, almost as long as the corolla, pale pink. **COROLLA** bell-shaped, 3–4mm long, hairless, slightly sticky, pale pink; lobes slightly spreading above, rounded. **ANTHERS** 8, concealed, with *toothed crests at the base* that are *completely joined to the filaments*. **STYLE** concealed, short and stout; stigma pinhead.

Colin Paterson-Jones

| J | F | M | A | M | J | J | A | S | O | N | D |

Peter Swart

Erica articularis

Cederberg to the Cape Peninsula and east along the coastal ranges to Humansdorp and inland on the Swartberg

FORM Upright, wand-like shrublet to 1(–2)m, *resprouting from a woody rootstock*, with erect branchlets often with numerous flowering spur-shoots in the axils so that the flowerheads form a dense plume up the length of the stems. **LEAVES** 3-whorled, pressed against the branches, needle-like or scale-like, with minute bristles along the margins. **FLOWERS** in 3s at the branch tips and on the reduced spur-shoots in the upper axils forming tight clusters, often massed in dense false-racemes, *on short stalks*; bracteoles scale-like. **SEPALS** large and leaf-shaped, more than half as long to almost as long as the corolla tube, overlapping in two pairs, papery, petal-like, white or pale pink. **COROLLA** urn-shaped with a narrow mouth, erect or spreading, 4mm long, hairless, *bright pink but soon turning brown*; lobes small and spreading, blunt or pointed. **ANTHERS** 8, concealed, with jagged crests at the base. **STYLE** concealed; stigma pinhead.

J	F	M	A	M	J	J	A	S	O	N	D

Nick Helme

Erica palliiflora

Cloaked Heath

Gravelly and sandy flats and slopes from the Cederberg to the Cape Peninsula and Bredasdorp and along the Langeberg and Outeniqua Mtns to George

FORM Upright, wand-like shrublet to 50cm, sometimes with short flowering branchlets arising successively up the stems so that the flowerheads form short false-racemes. **LEAVES** 3-whorled, *pressed against the stem*, needle-like or awl-like, minutely velvety on the upper surface. **FLOWERS** 1 to 3 on reduced spur-shoots at the tips of the branchlets, forming a cluster at the tops of the stems and also on short-shoots near the tops of the stems, aggregated into interrupted false-racemes, stalked; bracteoles scale-like, dry and papery, pink. **SEPALS** *large* and *narrowly leaf-shaped, ±as long as the corolla tube*, overlapping in two pairs, papery, petal-like and coloured like the corolla. **COROLLA** shortly tubular or urn-shaped, nodding, 4–5mm long, hairless, pale or pale pink and white; lobes small and slightly spreading, blunt. **ANTHERS** 8, concealed, with jagged crests at the base. **STYLE** reaching mouth of tube; stigma pinhead.

Includes forms previously known as *Erica chlamydiflora* and the white-flowered *Erica nivea*.

Nicky van Berkel

John Manning

Ross Turner

Erica gnaphaloides

Marshy flats and lower slopes from the Franschhoek Mtns to the Kogelberg and Cape Peninsula

Very like *Erica palliiflora* (see p. 125) but with smaller flowers and a distinctive cross-shaped stigma with 4 short spreading arms.

FORM Upright, wand-like shrublet to 40cm, sometimes with short flowering branchlets arising successively up the stems so that the flowerheads form short false-racemes. **LEAVES** 3-whorled, *pressed against the stem*, needle-like or awl-like, minutely velvety on the upper surface. **FLOWERS** 1 to 3 on reduced spur-shoots at the tips of the branchlets, forming a cluster at the tops of the stems and also on short-shoots near the tops of the stems, aggregated into interrupted false-racemes, on stalks covered with glands; bracteoles needle-like. **SEPALS** *large and broadly leaf-shaped, ±as long as the corolla tube*, overlapping in two pairs, papery, petal-like and coloured like the corolla. **COROLLA** urn-shaped or bell-shaped, nodding, 2.5–3mm long, hairless, pink; lobes small and slightly spreading, blunt. **ANTHERS** 8, concealed, with jagged crests at the base. **STYLE** reaching mouth of tube, *cross-shaped with four short, spreading arms*.

Corinne Merry

Nick Helme

Corinne Merry

Erica totta

Rocky slopes, sometimes dominant, from the Cederberg along the western ranges to Somerset West

This species was previously placed among the 'minor' genera as *Eremia totta* due to its indehiscent fruits.

FORM Mat-forming or spreading shrublet to 30cm tall and 1m across, with numerous erect additional flowering branchlets.
LEAVES 3-whorled, needle-like, *minutely hairy* and *appearing greyish*, with *white bristly hairs on the underside and margins*. **FLOWERS** in 1 or 2 whorls at the tips of the branchlets, aggregated into dense, spike-like clusters, stalkless or on short stalks, with a sour fragrance; *bracteoles pressed against the calyx, large* and *papery* with *fringed margins, white*. **SEPALS** large and elliptical, papery and petal-like, hairless or minutely hairy, *conspicuously fringed on the margins*. **COROLLA** urn-shaped and 4-keeled or -winged at the base, 2.5–4mm long, hairless or minutely hairy, *white but soon turning brown*; lobes erect, rounded.
ANTHERS 8, concealed, *rounded at the base*. **STYLE** reaching just beyond the mouth of the tube; stigma pinhead.
FRUIT not splitting open, papery or brittle.

| J | F | M | A | M | J | J | A | S | O | N | D |

John Manning

John Manning

Oswald Kurten

Cluster 4 ■ BEAKED HEATHS
Corolla lobes hard and pointed, forming a sharp beak, and with large, petal-like sepals

Erica spumosa
Frothy Heath, Swartbekkie

Damp sandy flats and slopes or seeps on the Cape Peninsula and the Hottentots Holland and Riviersonderend Mtns to Bredasdorp

FORM Upright shrublet to 45cm, with numerous short flowering branchlets or short-shoots. **LEAVES** 3-whorled, almost scale-like, thick and waxy. **FLOWERS** mostly in 3s in *dainty, drooping heads nested among the leaves at the tips of the short-shoots*, aggregated into sparse or dense false-racemes, nodding, stalkless; bracteoles pressed against the calyx, large and petal-like, membranous and glossy, rather loose, coloured like the corolla. **SEPALS** large and petal-like, almost as long as the corolla and concealing it, overlapping in two opposite pairs, *membranous* and *glossy, keeled at the tips*, rather loose, *coloured like the corolla*. **COROLLA** cup- or bell-shaped, *3–4mm* long, *hairless*, white or pink; lobes erect and forming a beak, overlapping one another at the base with the sides somewhat folded inwards above. **ANTHERS** 8, *almost completely protruding* but *dropping off at an early stage*, black, pointed at the tips and *tapered at the base* with *tails almost completely joined to the filaments*. **STYLE** protruding well beyond the anthers; stigma pinhead.

J | F | M | A | M | J | J | A | S | O | N | D

Erica cumuliflora

Drier middle slopes from Grabouw along the Kleinrivier Mtns to Potberg

FORM Upright, widely branching shrublet to 50cm, with short, closely leafy flowering branches that are nodding at the tips. **LEAVES** 4-whorled, needle-like, with large glands along the margins. **FLOWERS** *5 to 12 in a tight, nodding head* at the tips of the branches, on short stalks; bract and bracteoles loosely pressed against the calyx, large and petal-like, dry and papery, roughly velvety towards the base and with minute hairs along the margins, white. **SEPALS** large and petal-like, as long as the corolla tube, *dry* and *papery, roughly velvety* and with *minute hairs and glands along the rather jagged or toothed margins*, white. **COROLLA** urn-shaped, *4–5mm* long, *hard and dry, rough and sandpaper-like or velvety, white* with *dark brown lobes*; lobes erect and converging to form a sharp beak, leaf-shaped but narrowed at the base into a short neck that is fringed with short hairs, otherwise smooth and hairless. **ANTHERS** 8, *concealed within the tube, rounded at the base*. **STYLE** *protruding just beyond the tips of the corolla lobes* and *slightly swollen* towards the end; stigma minute.

Ross Turner

J | F | M | A | M. | J | **J** | **A** | **S** | O | N | D

SIMILAR SPECIES *Erica genistifolia* from the Cape Peninsula and the Kleinrivier Mtns differs in its 3-whorled leaves and smaller heads of mostly 3 (rarely up to 6) flowers.

Ross Turner

Erica recurvata CRITICALLY RARE   Red-tipped Clusterflower Heath

Rock crevices on the Soetmuisberg above Napier

Like ***Erica cumuliflora*** (see p. 129) but a more compact shrublet to 50cm, ***resprouting from a woody rootstock***, with larger flowers, the corolla ***7–9mm*** long, with the ***crimson-red style protruding well beyond (5mm) the tips of the corolla lobes*** and slender throughout.

> This extraordinary species was described and illustrated in 1810 from plants cultivated in England. It remained an enigma and was thought by many to be a garden hybrid until erica researcher Ross Turner rediscovered it in the wild on 30 August 2007. It is still known only from this single small population.

J | F | M | A | M | J | **J** | **A** | **S** | O | N | D

Ross Turner

Ross Turner

Flowers usually in tight, nodding heads, with a woolly or silky calyx and/or corolla

Erica bruniifolia

Brunia-leaved Heath

Stony flats and lower slopes, sometimes on clay, from Grabouw to Bredasdorp and Potberg

FORM Upright shrublet to 50cm, with slender, ascending, closely leafy flowering branches that are nodding at the tips. **LEAVES** 3-, 4- or 6-whorled or scattered, erect and frequently curved inwards or spreading, needle-like, fringed with minute hairs or conspicuous bristles along the margins. **FLOWERS** many in tight, nodding heads at the tips of the branches, on short stalks or ±stalkless; bract and bracteoles pressed against the calyx, needle-like, the bract larger and longer than the sepals, with minute hairs or bristles along the margins and with long bristles towards the tips. **SEPALS** *needle-like*, ±as long as the corolla tube, with *short hairs or long bristles along the margins* and with *long bristles at the tips*, whitish. **COROLLA** egg- or urn-shaped, 3–4mm long, *hairless*, whitish; lobes erect, rounded. **ANTHERS** 8, almost or fully protruding, tapering at the base. **STYLE** protruding beyond the anthers; stigma pinhead.

| J | F | M | A | M | J | J | A | S | O | N | D |

Erica bruniades

Kapok Heath, Kapokkie

Widely distributed on damp sandy or peaty flats beside streams along the coast and in the western mountains from near Vanrhynsdorp to the Cape Peninsula and to Bredasdorp

FORM Upright, rounded or spreading shrublet to 45cm, with numerous short flowering branchlets sometimes bearing additional short-shoots. **LEAVES** 3-whorled, needle-like, densely hairy with a mix of short velvety hairs and long silky hairs, but these soon abrading off. **FLOWERS** mostly in 3s at the tips of the short-shoots, and aggregated into sparse or dense false-racemes, nodding on densely silky stalks; bracteoles scale-like, densely silky. **SEPALS** *lance-shaped*, almost as long as the corolla, white to deep pink, *densely covered with long, white or pink silky or woolly hairs*. **COROLLA** bell-shaped, 3–4mm long, *densely silky except for the lobes*, white or pink; lobes erect or spreading at the tips, rounded. **ANTHERS** 8, almost completely protruding, tapered at the base and pointed at the tips, shortly bristly. **STYLE** protruding well beyond the anthers; stigma pinhead.

| J | F | M | A | M | J | J | A | S | O | N | D |

Nick Helme

Colin Paterson-Jones

Colin Paterson-Jones

Colin Paterson-Jones

Erica lanata

Outeniqua and Tsitsikamma Mtns from George to Humansdorp

FORM Upright shrublet to 1m, with numerous short flowering branchlets sometimes bearing additional short-shoots. **LEAVES** 4-whorled, needle-like or more leaf-shaped with a broad gap exposing the lower surface, densely hairy with a mix of short velvety hairs and long silky hairs, but these soon abrading off. **FLOWERS** *mostly 4 to 6(10)* in little nodding heads at the tips of the flowering branchlets, ±stalkless; bracteoles paddle-like, pressed against and ±as long as the calyx, densely silky. **SEPALS** *needle-like*, almost as long as the corolla, *densely silky*. **COROLLA** bell-shaped, 3–4mm long, *velvety*, white; lobes erect, pointed. **ANTHERS** 8, almost completely protruding, tapered at the base and pointed at the tips, shortly bristly. **STYLE** protruding well beyond the anthers; stigma pinhead.

J F M A M J J A S O N D

Nicky van Berkel

Ross Turner

Erica sphaerocephala

Round-headed Heath

Along the western mountains from the Cederberg to the Hex River Mtns and the Piketberg

FORM Upright shrublet to 30cm, with numerous short flowering branchlets. **LEAVES** (3-)4-whorled or scattered, needle-like, densely hairy with a mix of short velvety hairs on the upper surface, more shaggy hairs on the lower surface, and long feather-like bristles along the margins, but sometimes almost hairless with age. **FLOWERS** *10 to 28* in tight, nodding heads at the tips of the flowering branchlets, ±stalkless, the *upper leaves and floral bracts sometimes forming a 'cape'* around the bottom of the head; bracts like the leaves and bracteoles small and needle-like, fringed with bristle-like hairs. **SEPALS** *small* and *lance-shaped, membranous, fringed with bristle-like or long feathery hairs* along the margins with a long bristle at the tip, coloured like the corolla. **COROLLA** *urn-shaped, 4–10mm* long, *hairless*, white to pale or deep pink or almost red; lobes erect, rounded. **ANTHERS** 8, concealed, *horned or crested at the base*. **STYLE** reaching just beyond the mouth; stigma pinhead.

> Larger-flowered plants with a corolla 5–10mm long were previously treated as the separate species *Erica maderi*.

J	F	M	A	M	J	J	A	S	O	N	D

SIMILAR SPECIES *Erica pudens* from the Kamiesberg in Namaqualand and the western mountains from the Cederberg to the Elandskloof Mtns south of Porterville is a sprawling species with a mix of long, gland-tipped bristles and short velvety hairs on the leaves, bracteoles and sepals, and white flowers with a conspicuously protruding style.

Erica cernua

Marshy soils and seepages on middle to upper slopes of the western mountains from the Cederberg and Koue Bokkeveld Mtns to the Groot Winterhoek above Porterville and Tulbagh

FORM Upright shrublet to 80cm, with numerous short, flowering branchlets. **LEAVES** 4-whorled, needle-like, erect or pressed against the stems, minutely velvety when young and with branched or feather-like hairs or bristles along the margins and sometimes an awn-like bristle at the tip, but sometimes almost hairless with age, the **upper leaves and floral bracts sometimes forming a 'cape'** around the bottom of the head. **FLOWERS 4 to 8** in tight, nodding heads at the tips of the flowering branchlets, ±stalkless; bracts like the leaves and bracteoles small and needle-like, fringed with feather-like hairs. **SEPALS larger than the leaves, lance-shaped and leathery, velvety and fringed with feather-like hairs or bristles** along the margins and tipped with a slender bristle, coloured like the corolla. **COROLLA urn-shaped or egg-shaped, abruptly narrowed to a small mouth, 5mm long, hairless**, pale to rosy pink; lobes erect, rounded. **ANTHERS** 8, concealed, with **jagged white crests at the base**. **STYLE** reaching just beyond the mouth; stigma pinhead.

| J | F | M | A | M | J | J | A | S | O | N | D |

Cluster 6 ▆ VELVETY HEATHS
Corolla velvety with the stamens and style concealed or protruding

Erica hirta
Hairy Heath

Dry lower slopes of the southwestern mountains on the Paardeberg south of Malmesbury and from Drakenstein to the Hottentots Holland Mtns

FORM Upright shrublet to 1.5m, sometimes *resprouting from a woody rootstock*, with ascending branchlets and spreading short-shoots, the branchlets covered with short velvety hairs mixed with long, gland-tipped bristles. **LEAVES** usually rather sparse, 3-whorled, spreading, *elliptical* with *most of the lower surface exposed*, covered with *gland-tipped bristles*. **FLOWERS** mostly in 3s at the tips of the branchlets and short-shoots, sometimes aggregated into large panicles, spreading on long, slender stalks covered with gland-tipped bristles; bracteoles scale-like, covered with short velvety hairs and gland-tipped bristles. **SEPALS** *lance-shaped*, covered with *short velvety hairs* and *gland-tipped bristles*. **COROLLA** globe-shaped and sharply contracted to the small mouth, *5–7mm* long, velvety and slightly sticky, white to pale pink; lobes slightly spreading at the ends, rounded. **ANTHERS** 8, concealed or partly protruding, with *hairy tails at the base*. **STYLE** shortly protruding; stigma pinhead.

This species was previously known as *Erica sphaeroidea*, and before that *Erica globosa*.

| J | F | M | A | M | J | J | A | S | O | N | D |

Erica caterviflora ENDANGERED

Damp peaty ledges and cliff faces on Table Mountain on the Cape Peninsula

FORM Upright shrublet or shrub to 4m, with ascending branchlets and numerous spreading short-shoots. **LEAVES** 4-whorled, needle-like, *shortly and stiffly hairy or bristly* (rarely hairless). **FLOWERS** 4 to 12 in tight clusters at the tips of the branchlets and short-shoots and aggregated into dense panicles, nodding on short stalks; bracteoles scale-like, bristly. **SEPALS** *leaf-shaped, bristly*. **COROLLA** urn-shaped, sharply 4-angled at the base between the sepals, *4–5mm* long, shortly and stiffly hairy or bristly, pink; lobes spreading, rounded. **ANTHERS** 8, concealed, with *large, hairy crests*. **STYLE** concealed; stigma pinhead.

This species was thought to be extinct but was rediscovered in 2006 and several small populations are now known from the Back Table. Plants with a hairy corolla are treated as var. *caterviflora* and rare individuals with a hairless corolla as var. *glabrata*.

J | F | M | A | M | J | J | A | S | O | N | D

Ross Turner

Nigel Forshaw

Erica hirtiflora

Hairy-flowered Heath

Moist slopes on the Cape Peninsula

FORM Upright shrublet to 1m, with ascending branchlets and numerous additional short-shoots. **LEAVES** 4-whorled, needle-like, *shortly and stiffly hairy or bristly*. **FLOWERS** mostly in 4s at the tips of the branchlets and short-shoots and aggregated into panicles, nodding on short stalks; bracteoles scale-like. **SEPALS** *needle-like, bristly*. **COROLLA** urn-shaped, *3–5mm* long, shortly and stiffly hairy or bristly, pink to magenta; lobes erect or curving outwards, rounded. **ANTHERS** 8, concealed, with *long, hairy, yellow tails at the base*. **STYLE** concealed; stigma pinhead.

J	F	M	A	M	J	J	A	S	O	N	D

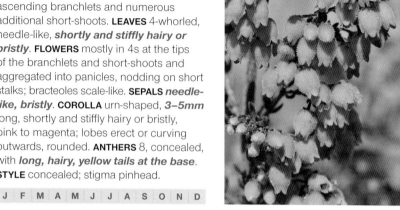

Erica mollis

Soft Heath

Moist places alongside streams on the Cape Peninsula mountains

Like **Erica hirtiflora** (above) but distinguished from it by the flowers being more closely aggregated in dense false-racemes or panicles, with a globe-shaped corolla, and especially the *enlarged, saucer-like stigma*.

J	F	M	A	M	J	J	A	S	O	N	D

Erica parviflora

Small-flowered Heath

Rocky slopes or flats, often alongside streams, from Wellington to the Cape Peninsula to Bredasdorp

FORM Upright shrublet to 90cm, with ascending branchlets and numerous additional short-shoots. **LEAVES** 3- or 4-whorled but becoming scattered above, needle-like, *shortly hairy*. **FLOWERS** mostly in 3s at the tips of the branchlets and short-shoots and aggregated into dense or interrupted panicles, nodding on short stalks; bracteoles scale-like. **SEPALS** *needle-like, shortly hairy*. **COROLLA** urn-shaped, *2–4mm* long, shortly hairy or velvety, pink to magenta; lobes erect or spreading at the tips, rounded. **ANTHERS** 8, concealed, with *smooth, needle-like tails at the base*. **STYLE** concealed; stigma pinhead, concealed.

| J | F | M | A | M | J | J | A | S | O | N | D |

John Manning

Ross Turner

Erica holosericea

Silky Heath

Cool southern slopes, often in the lee of rocks, from the Kogelberg along the Kleinrivier Mtns to Bredasdorp

FORM Upright shrublet to 90cm, with ascending branchlets bearing short-shoots in the upper axils. **LEAVES** 3-whorled, needle-like, *up to 15mm* long, *sharply pointed, fringed* with *whisker-like hairs along the margins* when young. **FLOWERS** in 3s at the tips of the branches and short-shoots and aggregated into loose clusters or false-racemes, nodding on slender stalks; bracteoles scale-like, velvety. **SEPALS** *large and lance-shaped, loosely clasping the corolla, petal-like, overlapping in two opposite pairs, more than half as long as the corolla, velvety, drying to form a hard ball around the fruit*. **COROLLA** bell-shaped, *5–10mm* long, velvety or sometimes hairless, pink to magenta, rather deeply lobed; lobes erect, half to two-thirds the length of the tube, rounded. **ANTHERS** 8, concealed, with *crests at the base*. **STYLE** reaching the mouth of the tube, concealed; stigma pinhead.

| J | F | M | A | M | J | J | A | S | O | N | D |

Nick Helme

Cluster 7 ■ **THRUM HEATHS**
Corolla smooth and hairless, with the stamens conspicuously
protruding beyond the mouth

Erica petraea

Rock Heath

Dry, rocky slopes at mid- to high altitudes on the drier inland mountains of the
southern seaboard from the Swartberg, Kammanassie and northern slopes of the
Outeniqua Mtns eastwards through the Baviaanskloof and Groot Winterhoek Mtns
near Kariega to the Suurberg near Addo

FORM Upright or spreading shrublet to 40cm, with ascending branchlets that sometimes
have a few additional spur-shoots towards the top. **LEAVES** 3-whorled, erect and *pressed
against the stem, elliptical* and *almost scale-like*, with *glands along the margins*.
FLOWERS at the tips of the branchlets and in the uppermost axils, forming ovoid or head-
like clusters, and also on the spur-shoots, spreading or nodding on short stalks; bracts
and bracteoles lance-shaped, *pressed against the calyx*, with glands along the margins,
coloured like the corolla. **SEPALS** lance-shaped, with *glands along the margins, coloured
like the corolla*. **COROLLA** egg- or urn-shaped, 3–4mm long, hairless, pale to deep pink;
lobes erect, rounded. **ANTHERS** 8, mostly or fully protruding, *rough*, with *minute spurs
at the base* that are *hidden alongside the filaments* and thus *apparently rounded*.
STYLE protruding beyond anthers;
stigma pinhead.

J	F	M	A	M	J	J	A	S	O	N	D

Nicky van Berkel

Erica nutans
Showy Heath

Along the southern coastal region from
Riversdale to East London

FORM Upright, willowy shrublet or shrub
from 1–1.8m, with numerous flowering
branchlets arising successively up the stems
so that the flowers form dense plumes
and panicles up the length of the stems.
LEAVES 3-whorled, needle-like, ±hairless.
FLOWERS 1 to 3 at the tips of the short-
shoots, arranged in plume-like panicles,
suberect on stalks; bracteoles needle-like.
SEPALS needle-like. **COROLLA** urn-shaped or
almost tubular, 3–4mm long, hairless, pale
pink to reddish; lobes suberect, rounded.
ANTHERS 8, mostly fully protruding, *rough,
rounded at the base*. **STYLE** protruding
well beyond the anthers; stigma pinhead.

Sally Adams

This species was previously
known as *Erica deliciosa*.

J F M A M J J A S O N D

Erica glumiflora VULNERABLE
Bract-flowered Heath

Coastal dunes and lower slopes along the southern coast from George to Humansdorp

FORM Upright shrublet to 60cm, with ascending branchlets and numerous additional short-
shoots. **LEAVES** 3-whorled, needle-like, with *glands along the margins*. **FLOWERS** mostly
in 3s at the tips of the short-shoots, which
are in whorls and aggregated into dense
false-racemes, spreading or nodding,
±stalkless; *bracteoles lance-shaped
and keel-tipped, pressed against the
calyx*, with glands along the margins.
SEPALS *lance-shaped, large and keel-
tipped*, with *glands along the margins,
±as long as the corolla*. **COROLLA** globe- or
cup-shaped, *2–3mm* long, *concealed
by the sepals*, hairless, white to pale pink
or rarely deep pink; lobes erect, rounded.
ANTHERS 8, fully protruding, with horn-like
spurs at the base that are partly joined to the
filament. **STYLE** protruding beyond anthers,
sometimes curved; stigma disc-like, usually
with 4 small finger-like lobes in the centre.

Ross Turner

J F M A M J J A S O N D

Erica imbricata

Salt-and-pepper Heath

Widely distributed throughout the region from near Vanrhynsdorp to the Cape Peninsula and eastwards along the coastal ranges, as well as the mountains of the Little Karoo to Joubertina

FORM Upright, rounded or wand-like shrublet to 90cm, with ascending branchlets and numerous additional short-shoots. **LEAVES** 4-whorled, needle-like, microscopically hairy. **FLOWERS** mostly in 3s at the tips of the branchlets and short-shoots, and aggregated into dense false-racemes, nodding on short stalks; *bracteoles large and petal-like, papery, pressed against the calyx, coloured like the corolla.* **SEPALS** *large and petal-like, keel-tipped, papery, ±as long as and coloured like the corolla.* **COROLLA** urn-shaped or sometimes almost radish-shaped, 4-grooved, 2–3.5mm long, concealed by the sepals, hairless, *white*; lobes erect, rounded. **ANTHERS** 8, fully protruding, tapering at the base. **STYLE** protruding beyond anthers, sometimes curved; stigma pinhead.

Intermediate forms occur with pink-flowered *Erica placentiflora* (see p. 144), and the complex needs further study.

| J | F | M | A | M | J | J | A | S | O | N | D |

SIMILAR SPECIES *Erica penicilliformis* from the Riviersonderend, Langeberg and Outeniqua Mtns is distinguished by its anthers, with the tips drawn into a sharp point rather than bluntly rounded as in *Erica imbricata*.

Ross Turner

John Manning

Nick Helme

Erica lasciva

Lesser Salt-and-pepper Heath

Cape Peninsula at Kenilworth Racecourse and along the coast from Stanford to Albertinia

Like **Erica imbricata** (opposite) but distinguished by the **shorter style** with a **disc-like stigma, usually with 4 small finger-like lobes** in the centre.

J	F	M	A	M	J	J	A	S	O	N	D

Nick Helme

Ross Turner

Erica triceps

Three-flowered Heath

Southern coastal mountains from the Langeberg at Swellendam along the Outeniqua and Tsitsikamma Mtns to Humansdorp

Like **Erica imbricata** (opposite) but the **bracts and sepals clasp the corolla more loosely** than in that species and the **corolla is more broadly urn-shaped**, 2.5–5mm long, with the **lobes curled outwards** so that the mouth is open.

J	F	M	A	M	J	J	A	S	O	N	D

Rendert Hoekstra

Colin Paterson-Jones

Erica placentiflora

Widely distributed on sandy flats and rock sheets throughout the western mountains from the Cederberg to Bredasdorp but not on the Cape Peninsula

Intermediate forms occur with white-flowered *Erica imbricata* (see p. 142) and the complex needs further study.

Like **Erica imbricata** (see p. 142) but with a **pink globe- or turnip-shaped corolla** that is **distinctly flattened** and **2mm** long, **markedly 4-grooved below**, contracted and indented around the mouth rather like a doughnut, with the **lobes tightly clasping the stamens**.

J | F | M | A | M | J | J | A | S | O | N | D

Ross Turner

Nick Helme

John Manning

Cluster 8 ■ STICKY HEATHS

Corolla hairless and sticky, with the stamens and style concealed or the style reaching just beyond the mouth

Erica urna-viridis RARE

Jade-urn Heath, Sticky Green Heath, Groentaaiheide

Cape Peninsula from Steenberg to St James

J	F	M	A	M	J	J	A	S	O	N	D

FORM Upright, sparsely branched shrublet to 1m with scattered branchlets or short-shoots.
LEAVES 3- or 4-whorled, needle-like, minutely toothed along the margins. **FLOWERS** 3 or 4(6) at the tips of a few, short branchlets towards the ends of the stems, occasionally aggregated in a whorl, nodding on long stalks; bracteoles scale-like. **SEPALS** lance-shaped, hairless. **COROLLA** urn-shaped, *8–12mm* long, hairless and *very sticky, pale green*; lobes slightly spreading, blunt. **ANTHERS** 8, concealed, with jagged horns at the base. **STYLE** concealed; stigma pinhead.

Nick Helme

Erica physodes

Bladder Heath, Sticky White Heath

Rocky sandstone slopes on the Cape Peninsula

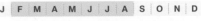

J	F	M	A	M	J	J	A	S	O	N	D

FORM Upright, sparsely branched shrublet to 1m, with scattered branchlets or short-shoots.
LEAVES 3- or 4-whorled, needle-like, minutely toothed along the margins. **FLOWERS** 3 or 4 at the tips of a few, short branchlets towards the ends of the stems, nodding on long stalks; bracteoles scale-like. **SEPALS** lance-shaped.
COROLLA urn-shaped, *7–8mm* long, hairless and *very sticky, white*; lobes slightly spreading, blunt. **ANTHERS** 8, concealed, with jagged horns at the base.
STYLE concealed; stigma pinhead.

John Manning

Erica ardens

Burning-ember Heath, Riversdale Bridal Heath

Langeberg Mtns from Swellendam to Heidelberg

FORM Upright, sparsely branched shrublet to 90cm, with wand-like stems bearing scattered branchlets or short-shoots. **LEAVES** 3(4)-whorled, needle-like, *minutely toothed* with *scattered glands along the margins*.
FLOWERS 1 to 3 at the tips of a few short-shoots towards the ends of the stems, occasionally aggregated in a whorl, nodding on short stalks; bracteoles lance-shaped. **SEPALS** *large* and *lance-shaped or petal-like*, rather loose with the *margins rolled in, sticky* with glands along the margins and on the inner surface, *reddish*. **COROLLA** urn-shaped and almost bladder-like, constricted at the top of the tube into a very small mouth, *6–8mm* long, hairless and *very sticky, scarlet*; lobes erect, rounded. **ANTHERS** 8, concealed, with jagged crests at the base. **STYLE** concealed; stigma pinhead.

Nick Helme

| J | F | M | A | M | J | J | A | S | O | N | D |

Erica obliqua

Oblique Heath

Damp flats and slopes on the Cape Peninsula and eastwards along the coastal ranges to Bredasdorp

FORM Upright shrublet with a solitary unbranched or sparsely branched stem to 40cm. **LEAVES** closely overlapping and scattered, not whorled, needle-like, minutely velvety on the upper surface and with a *large gland at the tip*. **FLOWERS** *12 to 20 in an umbel at the tip of the stem*, nodding on slender stalks; bracteoles scale-like, glandular. **SEPALS** small and needle- or scale-like, *covered with glands, dark red*. **COROLLA** urn-shaped or almost globe-shaped and constricted to a small mouth, *fluted* and *bulging longitudinally, 7–8mm* long, covered with *minute spicules*, sticky, reddish; lobes relatively large, erect or slightly spreading, blunt. **ANTHERS** 8, concealed, with toothed crests at the base. **STYLE** concealed; stigma pinhead.

> The minute spicules on the corolla are very difficult to see and the flowers appear to be hairless.

Nick Helme

| J | F | M | A | M | J | J | A | S | O | N | D |

Erica ferrea ENDANGERED

Iron-red Heath

Sandy flats and lower slopes of the southwestern coastal areas from Yzerfontein to Bellville and on the southern Cape Peninsula

Includes forms previously known as *Erica crenata*.

J	F	M	A	M	J	J	A	S	O	N	D

FORM Upright, slender shrublet to 40cm, with numerous flowering branchlets and additional short-shoots. **LEAVES** (3)4-whorled, needle-like, *minutely toothed with glands along the margins*. **FLOWERS** in *small umbels at the tips of the flowering branches* and short-shoots, aggregated into compound panicles, nodding on slender purple stalks; bracteoles needle-like. **SEPALS** *lance-shaped* and *papery* with a *firm tip, ±half as long as the corolla*, with *large glands* along the margins, *reddish*. **COROLLA** urn-shaped to almost globe-shaped and constricted to a small mouth, *3–5mm* long, hairless, glossy and sticky, reddish; lobes small, erect, rounded. **ANTHERS** 8, concealed, with large toothed crests at the base. **STYLE** concealed; stigma pinhead.

Nick Halme

Erica multumbellifera

Balloon Heath

Wettish slopes and flats from Tulbagh to the Cape Peninsula and eastwards along the coastal ranges to Riversdale

J	F	M	A	M	J	J	A	S	O	N	D

FORM Upright, slender shrublet to 40cm, with numerous flowering branchlets and additional short-shoots. **LEAVES** 4-whorled, needle-like. **FLOWERS** in *small umbels at the tips of the flowering branches* and short-shoots, aggregated into compound panicles, nodding on slender red stalks; bracteoles scale-like. **SEPALS** small and needle-like or scale-like. **COROLLA** *globe-shaped* and *sharply constricted or nipped into a small mouth*, sometimes fluted, *3–4mm* long, hairless, slightly sticky, reddish; lobes small, erect, rounded. **ANTHERS** 8, concealed, with toothed crests at the base. **STYLE** concealed; stigma pinhead.

Nick Helme

Erica spectabilis
White Limestone Heath

Coastal limestone hills on the Agulhas Plain from Bredasdorp to Gouritsmond west of Mossel Bay

> The replacement name *Erica doxantha* is being proposed for this species.

| J | F | M | A | M | J | J | A | S | O | N | D |

FORM Upright, twiggy shrublet to 60cm, with numerous flowering branchlets and sometimes additional short-shoots. **LEAVES** 3-whorled, *pressed against the stem* and *closely overlapping, scale-like, thick and glossy*, fringed with *stalked glands along the margins*. **FLOWERS** mostly in 3s at the tips of the branchlets and short-shoots, nodding on hairy and glandular stalks; bracts and bracteoles scale-like, dry and papery and keel-tipped. **SEPALS** *lance-shaped* and *papery* with a *firm tip, fringed with stalked glands along the margins, white*. **COROLLA** globe-shaped and constricted to a small mouth, *2–4mm* long, hairless, slightly sticky, *white*; lobes small, erect, rounded. **ANTHERS** 8, concealed, with *horns at the base that are partially joined to the filaments*. **STYLE** just reaching the mouth of the corolla; stigma pinhead.

Nick Helme

Erica syngenesia
Ring Heath

Drier inland mountains of the Little Karoo, on the Anysberg, Witteberg and Swartberg Mtns

FORM Upright, twiggy shrublet to 60cm, with numerous flowering branchlets and additional short-shoots. **LEAVES** 3-whorled, *pressed against the stem* and *closely overlapping, scale-like, velvety* and with *stalked glands along the margins*. **FLOWERS** mostly in 3s at the tips of the branchlets and short, nodding on velvety and glandular stalks; bracteoles scale-like, dry and papery and keel-tipped. **SEPALS** *lance-shaped* and *papery* with a *firm tip, minutely velvety* and with *stalked glands along the margins, white*. **COROLLA** urn-shaped and narrowed to a small mouth, *5mm* long, hairless, slightly sticky, *white*; lobes small, erect, rounded. **ANTHERS** 8, concealed, with *horns at the base* that are *partially joined to the ribbon-like filaments*. **STYLE** just reaching the mouth of the corolla; stigma pinhead.

Sandra Falanga

| J | F | M | A | M | J | J | A | S | O | N | D |

148 ■ **GROUP 3** SMALL-FLOWER HEATHS ■ **Cluster 8** STICKY HEATHS

Erica glomiflora

Coastal flats to middle slopes along the southern mountains from Mossel Bay to Humansdorp and inland from the Swartberg to the Kouga Mtns

FORM Upright, wand-like shrublet to 1m, with numerous short-shoots and flowering branchlets arising successively up the branches so that the flowers form a dense plume up the length of the stems. **LEAVES** 3-whorled, needle-like, hairless or shortly bristly. **FLOWERS** in 3s on the short-shoots, arranged in *dense, plume-like false-racemes* towards the ends of the branches, stalked; bracteoles lance-shaped, dry and papery. **SEPALS** *leaf-shaped, dry* and *papery, coloured like the corolla*. **COROLLA** urn-shaped with a short neck and narrow mouth, spreading or slightly nodding, *5–8(–10)mm* long, hairless, slightly sticky, white or pink to magenta; lobes spreading above, rounded. **ANTHERS** 8, concealed, with *long hairy tails at the base* that are *partially joined to the filaments*. **STYLE** concealed or reaching just beyond the mouth of the tube; stigma pinhead.

J	F	M	A	M	J	J	A	S	O	N	D

D. Underwood

Colin Paterson-Jones

Colin Paterson-Jones

Erica formosa

White Heath, Witheide

Cool lower slopes, often in seepages along the southern coastal region from Mossel Bay to Humansdorp

FORM Upright, densely branched shrublet to 60cm, with numerous flowering branchlets arising successively up the branches so that the flowers form dense plumes and panicles up the length of the stems. **LEAVES** 3-whorled, short and almost scale-like. **FLOWERS** in 3s on the short-shoots, *arranged in loose, plume-like false-racemes* towards the ends of the branches, aggregated into panicles, stalked; bracteoles near the top of the flower stalk just beneath the calyx, lance-shaped, dry and papery. **SEPALS** *leaf-shaped, dry* and *papery, coloured like the corolla.* **COROLLA** globe-shaped with a narrow mouth, *longitudinally 4-fluted* with *slight bulging sides*, nodding, *4mm* long, hairless, slightly sticky, white; lobes suberect, rounded. **ANTHERS** 8, concealed, with *long hairy tails at the base* that are *partially joined to the filaments*. **STYLE** concealed; stigma pinhead.

J | F | M | A | M | J | J | A | S | O | N | D

Nicky van Berkel

Nicky van Berkel

Sandra Falanga

Cluster 9 ■ DRY HEATHS
Corolla hairless and dry, with the stamens and style concealed or the style reaching just beyond the mouth

9a	GLANDULAR HEATHS Leaves sticky with gland-tipped hairs

Erica bicolor
Bicoloured Heath

Along the western mountains from the Gifberg near Vanrhynsdorp through the Cederberg to Paarl and the Stellenbosch Mtns

FORM Upright, wand-like shrublet to 90cm, with numerous erect flowering branchlets and additional short-shoots. **LEAVES** 3-whorled, spreading, needle-like, *velvety* and with *additional longer stalked glands*, especially along the margins. **FLOWERS** mostly in 3s at the tips of the branchlets and short-shoots, aggregated into open panicles, nodding on velvety and glandular-haired stalks; bracteoles scale-like, velvety and with reddish gland tipped bristles along the margins. **SEPALS** *leaf-shaped, velvety* and with *reddish gland-tipped bristles* along the margins, *pink with a small green tip*. **COROLLA** *cup-shaped* and *open* with a *distinctive rounded, bowl-like base*, 3mm long and as wide, hairless, pink or mauve; lobes relatively large, erect, ±pointed. **ANTHERS** 8, reaching the top of the tube and exposed in the open mouth, with horns at the base. **STYLE** protruding well beyond the anthers; stigma pinhead.

J	F	M	A	M	J	J	A	S	O	N	D

Erica scabriuscula

Shady kloofs and gulleys in moist places along the southern coastal ranges from Mossel Bay to Humansdorp

FORM Upright, rather willowy shrub to 2m, with ascending branchlets bearing numerous additional short-shoots, the branchlets covered with short velvety hairs mixed with long, gland-tipped bristles. **LEAVES** (3-)4-whorled or scattered, spreading, needle-like or almost elliptical, *covered with gland-tipped bristles*. **FLOWERS** mostly in 4s at the tips of the branchlets and short-shoots, and aggregated into plume-like panicles, spreading on short stalks; bracteoles scale-like, covered with gland-tipped bristles. **SEPALS** *needle-like, covered with gland-tipped bristles*. **COROLLA** urn-shaped, 3–4mm long, hairless, white to pale or rosy pink; lobes erect, rounded. **ANTHERS** 8, concealed, with tails at the base. **STYLE** shortly protruding; stigma pinhead.

Sally Adams

Includes forms previously known as *Erica gibbosa*.

| J | F | M | A | M | J | J | A | S | O | N | D |

9b CUP-FLOWERED HEATHS Flowers cup-shaped, not evidently narrowed at the mouth

Erica capensis RARE

Marshy flats in the Cape of Good Hope section of Table Mountain National Park

FORM Upright, rounded shrublet to 50cm, with numerous flowering branchlets and additional short-shoots. **LEAVES** 4-whorled, needle-like. **FLOWERS** mostly in 4s at the tips of the branchlets and short-shoots, aggregated into dense compound panicles, nodding on short, *hairless stalks*; bracteoles scale-like. **SEPALS** small and needle-like or scale-like. **COROLLA** *cup-shaped, 4–5mm* long, hairless, white or pale to dark pink; lobes small, erect, blunt. **ANTHERS** 8, concealed, with small crests at the base. **STYLE** reaching just beyond the mouth of the tube; stigma pinhead.

| J | F | M | A | M | J | J | A | S | O | N | D |

SIMILAR SPECIES *Erica eburnea*, also from marshy places on the Cape Peninsula, has slightly smaller, white flowers with the corolla 3mm long and scarcely longer than the sepals. It may be merely a form of *Erica capensis*.

Nick Helme

Erica paniculata

Lower slopes, often on loamy and granitic soils, in fynbos or transitional renosterveld from Tulbagh to the Hottentots Holland Mtns and the Cape Peninsula

FORM Upright shrublet to 50cm, the *branches felted with feathery hairs* and bearing numerous flowering spur-shoots successively up the stems, forming dense, narrow plumes. **LEAVES** 3-whorled, overlapping, needle-like, with *minute tufted hairs along the margins*. **FLOWERS** mostly in 3s at the tips of the short-shoots, aggregated into densely packed, plume-like false-racemes, nodding, stalked; bracteoles scale-like. **SEPALS** needle-like or scale-like, pink. **COROLLA** *cup-shaped* with an *open mouth, 2–2.5mm* long, hairless, pale pink; lobes erect or spreading, blunt. **ANTHERS** 8, reaching just beyond the top of the tube and exposed in the open mouth, *rounded at the base*. **STYLE** protruding well beyond the anthers; stigma pinhead or knob.

> The fresh flowers produce clouds
> of pollen when shaken.

J | F | M | A | M | J | J | A | S | O | N | D

FLORISTS' HEATHS

The following four species all have small, cup-shaped flowers 2.5–4mm long, and are easily confused. The general description applies to them all, and the individual descriptions highlight the characters that distinguish each one.

FORM Upright, rounded shrublet to 70cm, with numerous flowering branchlets and additional short-shoots. **LEAVES** 4-whorled, needle-like. **FLOWERS** mostly in 4s at the tips of the branchlets and short-shoots, aggregated into dense compound panicles, nodding on short stalks; bracteoles scale-like. **SEPALS** small and needle-like or scale-like. **COROLLA** *cup-shaped, 2.5–4mm* long, hairless, white or pale to dark pink; lobes small, erect, blunt. **ANTHERS** 8, concealed, with spurs or crests at the base. **STYLE** reaching just beyond the mouth of the tube; stigma pinhead.

❶ *Erica curvirostris*
Honey-scented Heath, Heuningheide

Seasonally moist slopes on the southwestern mountains from Bain's Kloof to the Hottentots Holland Mtns and the Cape Peninsula

> The flowers are strongly honey-scented.

J **F M A M** J J A S O N D

Flower stalks minutely velvety. **ANTHERS** oblong, longer than broad, with jagged or hairy crests at the base longer than the anther. **STYLE** sometimes extending beyond the corolla lobes and curved.

❷ *Erica subdivaricata*
Subdivaricate Heath

Seasonally moist lower slopes and flats on the southwestern coastal lowlands from Mamre to Bredasdorp
Flower stalks hairless. **ANTHERS** oblong,

> The flowers are strongly honey-scented.

J F **M A M J** J A S O N D

longer than broad, with slender, horn-like tails at the base slightly shorter than the anther.

❸ *Erica quadrangularis*
Florists' Heath

Widespread and common on seasonally wet slopes and flats throughout the southwestern mountains from the Cederberg to the Hottentots Holland Mtns and eastwards along the coastal ranges to the Outeniqua Mtns

> This species is widely cultivated and a favourite among florists. It includes plants previously known as *Erica cyathiformis*.

J F M A M **J J A S O N** D

Flower stalks hairless. **ANTHERS** short, as broad as long or slightly broader than long, with short, slender, horn-like tails at the base about half as long as the anther.

❹ *Erica mauritanica*
Keyhole Heath

Seasonally wet slopes and flats on the Cape Peninsula and the Stellenbosch and Hottentots Holland Mtns

> It is not clear if this species is distinct from *Erica quadrangularis* (above).

J F M A M J J **A S O N** D

Like ***Erica quadrangularis*** (above) but with the notches between the corolla lobes distinctly rounded at the bottom, forming keyholes or pinholes in the buds.

Erica curvirostris

Erica quadrangularis

Erica subdivaricata

Erica subdivaricata

Erica mauritanica

Erica bergiana

Bergius's Heath

Seeps and moist upper slopes on the southwestern mountains from the Koue Bokkeveld to the Hottentots Holland and Riversonderend Mtns

FORM Upright shrublet to 1m, with numerous flowering branchlets and additional short-shoots, the flowering branchlets covered with long spreading hairs or bristles. **LEAVES** 4-whorled, needle-like, *densely bristly*. **FLOWERS** mostly in 4s at the tips of the branchlets and short-shoots, aggregated into dense compound panicles, nodding on short stalks; bracteoles scale-like. **SEPALS** *distinctively flexed backwards*, lance-shaped with a needle-like tip, *fringed with short bristles along the margins*. **COROLLA** *globe-shaped* and *abruptly constricted to the small mouth*, 3–7mm long, hairless, pale to deep pink or reddish; lobes small, erect or curving outwards above, blunt. **ANTHERS** 8, concealed, with jagged crests at the base. **STYLE** reaching just beyond the mouth of the tube; stigma pinhead.

J F M A M J J A S O N D

John Manning

Nick Helme

Erica lateralis

Along the southwestern mountains from Tulbagh to the Kogelberg

FORM Upright to sprawling shrublet to 50cm, with reduced short-shoots or spur-shoots in the upper leaf axils. **LEAVES** 4-whorled, needle-like, hairless or velvety. **FLOWERS** mostly in 4s at the tips of the branches and the spur-shoots, aggregated into dense or loose false-racemes, nodding on short or slender stalks; bract and bracteoles scale-like or needle-like, *arising midway along the flower stalk*. **SEPALS** lance-shaped with a median groove, often minutely velvety, reddish. **COROLLA** urn-shaped, 4–10mm long, hairless, pale to deep rosy pink; lobes small, spreading in the upper part, blunt. **ANTHERS** 8, *concealed or just protruding beyond the mouth of the tube*, with pale crests at the base. **STYLE** reaching beyond the mouth of the tube; stigma pinhead.

J	F	M	A	M	J	J	A	S	O	N	D

Nick Helme

John Manning

Erica verecunda

Sandy flats and slopes along the western mountains, on the Kamiesberg in Namaqualand and from near Nieuwoudtville along the Cederberg to the Koue Bokkeveld north of Ceres and inland onto the Witteberg

FORM Upright to somewhat spreading shrub to 1.5m, with slender flowering branches and branchlets. **LEAVES** 4-whorled, needle-like, often rather scattered, microscopically hairy on the upper surface. **FLOWERS** *several in a cluster or umbel at the tips of the branchlets*, nodding on short or slender, reddish stalks, faintly honey-scented; bracteoles small or needle-like, *often pressed against the calyx*, reddish. **SEPALS** lance-shaped with a median groove, often minutely velvety, reddish. **COROLLA** urn-shaped, 2–6mm long, hairless, almost white to pale rosy pink; lobes small, spreading in the upper part, blunt. **ANTHERS** 8, concealed, with crests at the base. **STYLE** reaching just beyond the mouth of the tube; stigma pinhead.

John Manning

| J | F | M | A | M | J | J | A | S | O | N | D |

Nigel Forshaw

Erica laeta

Cheerful Heath

Marshy flats and lowlands on the Cape Peninsula and from Betty's Bay to Hermanus

FORM Upright, rounded shrublet to 50cm, with numerous flowering branchlets and additional short-shoots. **LEAVES** 4-whorled, needle-like. **FLOWERS** mostly in 4s at the tips of the branchlets and short-shoots, aggregated into dense compound panicles, nodding on short, *hairless stalks*; bracteoles scale-like. **SEPALS** small and needle-like or scale-like, *fringed with stalked glands along the margins*. **COROLLA** urn-shaped with a constricted mouth, 4–5mm long, hairless, rosy pink; lobes small, erect, blunt. **ANTHERS** 8, concealed, with jagged white crests at the base. **STYLE** reaching just beyond the mouth of the tube; stigma pinhead.

Ross Turner

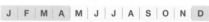

| J | F | M | A | M | J | J | A | S | O | N | D |

Nick Helme

Erica sitiens

Extreme southwestern mountains from the Hottentots Holland to the Kleinrivier Mtns

FORM Upright or sprawling shrublet to 90cm, with ascending branches bearing numerous flowering branchlets or spur-shoots in the axils so that the flowers form a dense plume up the length of the stems.

J	F	M	A	M	J	J	A	S	O	N	D

LEAVES *3-whorled*, needle-like. **FLOWERS** 1 to 4 at the branch tips and on the reduced spur-shoots, forming tight, narrow, plume-like panicles, on short stalks; bracteoles scale-like. **SEPALS** *large* and *needle-like* but *broader at the base*. **COROLLA** urn-shaped, spreading or nodding, *6–8mm* long, hairless, pale to deep pink, sometimes bicoloured with white tips, or plain white; lobes suberect, rounded. **ANTHERS** 8, concealed, with jagged tails or crests at the base. **STYLE** concealed; stigma pinhead.

Nick Helme

9d	**SPURRED HEATHS** Flowers urn-shaped; anthers with spurs or horns at the base

Erica intervallaris

Seepages and streamsides on mountain slopes in the Hottentots Holland, Kogelberg and Riviersonderend Mtns

FORM Upright or sprawling shrublet to 60cm, with numerous flowering branchlets and additional short-shoots. **LEAVES** 4-whorled, needle-like, covered with short hairs. **FLOWERS** mostly in 4s at the tips of the short-shoots, which are often in pairs or whorls and are aggregated into dense or long and interrupted false-racemes, nodding on short stalks; bracteoles scale-like. **SEPALS** *lance-shaped, somewhat papery, fringed with short hairs along the margins, coloured like the corolla*. **COROLLA** urn-shaped and 4-angled, 4mm long, usually hairless, reddish pink to purplish; lobes small, erect, blunt. **ANTHERS** 8, concealed, with spurs at the base. **STYLE** reaching just beyond the mouth of the tube; stigma pinhead.

J	F	M	A	M	J	J	A	S	O	N	D

Carina Becker

Erica subulata

Drier rocky and stony slopes from Ceres to Paarl and especially Du Toitskloof

FORM Upright, rounded shrublet to 1m, with numerous flowering branchlets and additional short-shoots, the branches velvety and with additional longer wispy hairs. **LEAVES** scattered but mostly opposite or 4-whorled on the flowering shoots, spreading or curved inwards, rather long, needle-like and tipped with a bristle. **FLOWERS** in *small clusters or heads at the tips of the branchlets* and short-shoots, nodding on short stalks; *bracts and bracteoles pressed against the calyx*, needle-like with slender tips. **SEPALS** long and needle-like from a broadened membranous base and *drawn into a wispy, hair-like tip*. **COROLLA** urn-shaped or shortly cylindrical with a small mouth, 4–5mm long, hairless, pale porcelain pink or tinged rose-pink at the tip; lobes small, erect, blunt. **ANTHERS** 8, concealed, with a distinct 'chin' and slender awns at the base. **STYLE** reaching just beyond the mouth of the tube; stigma pinhead.

> The pale wispy tips of the sepals are especially evident when the flowers are still in bud.

J	F	M	A	M	J	J	A	S	O	N	D

John Manning

Erica tenella

Extreme southwestern mountains from the Hottentots Holland and Kleinrivier Mtns to Elim

| J | F | M | A | M | J | J | A | S | O | N | D |

Magriet Brink

FORM Upright shrublet to 1m, with ascending branches bearing numerous flowering branchlets or spur-shoots in the axils so that the flowers form a dense plume up the length of the stems. **LEAVES** *3-whorled*, needle-like. **FLOWERS** 1 to 4 at the branch tips and on the reduced spur-shoots, forming tight, narrow, plume-like panicles, on short stalks; bracteoles scale-like. **SEPALS** large and needle-like but broader at the base, reddish. **COROLLA** urn-shaped, spreading or nodding, *4–6mm* long, hairless, bright to deep pink; lobes suberect, rounded. **ANTHERS** 8, *very short* and *either globe-shaped or wider than long*, concealed, tailed at the base. **STYLE** concealed; stigma pinhead.

Erica gracilis

Southern coastal lowlands from Heidelberg to Humansdorp

| J | F | M | A | M | J | J | A | S | O | N | D |

Sandra Falanga

FORM Upright, rounded shrublet to 70cm, with numerous flowering branchlets and additional short-shoots. **LEAVES** 4-whorled, needle-like. **FLOWERS** mostly in 4s at the tips of the branchlets and short-shoots, aggregated into dense compound panicles, nodding on short, *hairless stalks*; bracteoles scale-like. **SEPALS** *lance-shaped, overlapping in two opposite pairs*. **COROLLA** urn-shaped 3–4mm long, hairless, bright to rosy pink; lobes small, erect, blunt. **ANTHERS** 8, concealed, very small, with small horn-like tails at the base. **STYLE** reaching just beyond the mouth of the tube; stigma pinhead.

Flowers minute, cup-shaped, 1–1.5mm long, with 8 anthers and the mouth of the corolla ±blocked by a large, saucer-shaped stigma. (These species were previously placed in the genera *Philippia*, *Salaxis* and *Scyphogyne*. They are wind-pollinated.)

Erica hispidula — Bristly Heath

Widely distributed and common throughout the region from the Cederberg to the Cape Peninsula and eastwards to Kariega

FORM Upright, rounded shrublet or shrub to 1(–1.8)m, with ascending, *glandular-haired branchlets* bearing numerous short-shoots. **LEAVES** 3-whorled, needle-like, *usually microscopically hairy*. **FLOWERS** mostly in 3s at the tips of the short-shoots and aggregated into false-racemes, nodding on short stalks; bracteoles scale-like. **SEPALS** scale-like or needle-like. **COROLLA** bell-shaped, 1–1.5mm long, hairless, white to pink; lobes erect, rounded. **ANTHERS** 8, concealed, rounded at the base. **STYLE** protruding; stigma widened and saucer-shaped, reddish.

The flowers release clouds of pollen when brushed.

| J | F | M | A | M | J | J | A | S | O | N | D |

John Manning

Erica coarctata

Dry sandy or gravelly flats and lower slopes, scattered in the extreme southwestern lowlands from Tulbagh to the Cape Peninsula eastwards to Riversdale

FORM Erect, multi-stemmed shrublet to 30cm (rarely more), *resprouting from a woody base*. **LEAVES** 3(4)-whorled, needle-like, hairless. **FLOWERS** *1 or 2 in the upper axils on short scaly stalks*, forming *elongate spikes at the ends of the branches*, nodding on short stalks; bracteoles scale-like. **SEPALS** small and lance-shaped. **COROLLA** cup-shaped, scarcely longer than the calyx, 1–1.5mm long, hairless, greenish or flushed dull reddish; lobes erect, rounded. **ANTHERS** 8, ±concealed, rounded at the base. **STYLE** protruding, short or long and distinctly curved; stigma widened and saucer-shaped, reddish.

The pollen is readily shed in clouds when the plants are brushed.

J F **M A M J J A S** O N D

Ross Turner

Erica tristis
Mourning Heath

Sandy flats and rocky slopes, and prominent in areas that have escaped regular fires, in southwestern coastal districts from Langebaan to the Cape Peninsula eastwards to Gansbaai

> The pollen is readily shed in clouds when the plants are brushed.

| J | F | M | A | M | J | J | A | S | O | N | D |

FORM Upright, densely branched shrub or small tree, 1–3m, with numerous flowering branchlets bearing short-shoots. **LEAVES** 3-whorled, needle-like or scale-like, with glands along the margins. **FLOWERS** in 3s at the tips of the flowering branchlets and the short-shoots, which are often aggregated into interrupted false-racemes, on short, glandular stalks; bracts and bracteoles merged with the sepals and not evident. **SEPALS** *unequal*, with the *lower one larger and lance-shaped, others scale-like, leathery* with *glands on the margins*. **COROLLA** cup-shaped, 1–1.5mm long, hairless, dull cream-coloured; lobes erect, rounded. **ANTHERS** 8, concealed or just protruding, rounded at the base, the *filaments completely attached to the corolla*. **STYLE** protruding just beyond the anthers; stigma large and funnel-shaped, completely blocking the mouth of the corolla or shortly protruding above the anthers.

Erica axillaris
Trembling Heath

Sandy coastal flats and rocky slopes in southwestern coastal districts from Yzerfontein and Tulbagh to the Cape Peninsula eastwards to Knysna

| J | F | M | A | M | J | J | A | S | O | N | D |

FORM Upright shrublet to 1m, with numerous flowering branchlets bearing short-shoots. **LEAVES** 3-whorled, needle-like. **FLOWERS** in 3s at the tips of the flowering branchlets and the short-shoots, which are often aggregated into false-racemes, stalkless; *bracts and bracteoles merged with the sepals* and *not evident*. **SEPALS** *unequal*, with the *lower one larger and needle-like, others scale-like*. **COROLLA** cup-shaped, 1–1.5mm long, hairless or minutely hairy, yellowish or tinged red, soon becoming papery brown; lobes erect, rounded. **ANTHERS** 8, concealed, rounded at the base, the *filaments sometimes completely attached to the corolla*. **OVARY** 2- to 4-chambered. **STYLE** *obsolete*; stigma large and funnel-shaped, completely blocking the mouth of the corolla. **FRUIT** *not splitting open, hard* and *stone-like*.

Erica serrata

Hottentots Holland Mtns inland
to Riviersonderend and along the
Kleinrivier Mtns to Bredasdorp

FORM Upright shrublet to 1m, with numerous flowering branchlets bearing short-shoots. **LEAVES** 3-whorled, needle-like, hairless or minutely hairy, the *young leaves with large glands on the margins, which become toothed in older leaves*. **FLOWERS** 3 or 6 at the tips of the flowering branchlets and the short-shoots, which are often aggregated into false-racemes, ±stalkless; *bracts and bracteoles merged with the sepals* and *not evident*. **SEPALS** *unequal, joined in a cup* that is furrowed below, *the lowermost lobe largest, lance-shaped, others smaller*, all with *dark red to black glands* on the margins. **COROLLA** narrowly cup-shaped, 1.5mm long, hairless or minutely hairy in the upper half, greenish white; lobes erect, rounded. **ANTHERS** 8, concealed, rounded at the base, with the *filaments completely joined to the corolla*. **OVARY** *2-chambered*, the *lower third or half joined to the corolla*. **STYLE** *obsolete*; stigma large and saucer-shaped, completely blocking the mouth of the corolla. **FRUIT** partially splitting open, leathery.

| J | F | M | A | M | J | J | A | S | O | N | D |

Erica muscosa

Widely distributed on rocky slopes and sandy flats throughout the western and southern mountains from Nieuwoudtville to the Cape Peninsula and Bredasdorp eastwards along the Langeberg and Outeniqua Mtns to George; very common and sometimes dominant, but easily overlooked

FORM Upright shrublet to 0.5m or rarely 2m, with numerous flowering branchlets bearing short-shoots. **LEAVES** 3-whorled, ±spreading, needle-like, hairless or minutely hairy, *usually with a conspicuous large gland at the tip of the blade*. **FLOWERS** 3 or 6 at the tips of the flowering branchlets and the short-shoots, which are often aggregated into false-racemes, stalkless; *bracts and bracteoles merged with the sepals* and *not evident*. **SEPALS** *subequal, joined in a cup*, the lowermost lobe sometimes slightly larger, hairless or minutely hairy, yellowish. **COROLLA** cup-shaped, 1mm long, hairless, yellowish green becoming white; lobes erect, rounded. **ANTHERS** 8, shortly protruding and soon deciduous, thus the older flowers without anthers, rounded at the base. **OVARY** *1-chambered, tapering into a short style*. **STYLE** shortly protruding; stigma large and saucer-shaped with the *edges becoming scalloped* with age, level with the tops of the anthers and closely surrounded by them. **FRUIT** *not splitting open, papery*.

J	F	M	A	M	J	J	A	S	O	N	D

Ross Turner

Ross Turner

GROUP 5
MINOR HEATHS

Flowers up to 5mm long, pink to mauve, with 4 protruding anthers

Cluster 1 ■ BLAERIA HEATHS

Fruit woody and splitting open at maturity to shed the seeds, 4-chambered with several seeds per chamber; sepals ±separate to the base. (These species were previously placed in the genus *Blaeria*.)

Erica ericoides

Honey Heath

Rocky slopes and sandy flats, often in dense stands on the Cape Peninsula and the Kogelberg along the Kleinrivier Mtns to Stanford

FORM Upright, closely branched and compact shrublet to 70cm, with numerous flowering branchlets and short-shoots. **LEAVES** 4-whorled, needle-like, *sparsely and softly hairy*. **FLOWERS** in nodding, 6- to 12-flowered heads at the tips of the branchlets and short-shoots, clustered into panicles, on short stalks, strongly honey-scented; *bracteoles pressed against the calyx*, needle-like. **SEPALS** needle-like. **COROLLA** shortly tubular or bell-shaped, 2.5–4mm long, hairless but rough, pink; lobes erect or slightly spreading, with the margins rolled over, blunt. **ANTHERS** 4, completely protruding, *rounded or angled at the base*. **STYLE** protruding; stigma club-shaped.

This species was previously known as *Blaeria ericoides*.

| J | F | M | A | M | J | J | A | S | O | N | D |

Erica equisetifolia

Cape Peninsula and throughout the southwestern mountains from Bain's Kloof to Bredasdorp

FORM Upright, compact shrublet to 30cm, with *numerous erect, whip-like flowering branchlets*. **LEAVES** 3-whorled, erect and closely pressed against the stems, needle-like. **FLOWERS** in nodding, 3- to 9-flowered heads at the tips of the branchlets and often also on a few reduced short-shoots just below the branch tips, stalked; *bracteoles on the upper part of the stalks*, needle-like or scale-like. **SEPALS** *joined in a short cup*, needle-like. **COROLLA** narrowly cup-shaped to shortly tubular and 4-angled, 2.5–4mm long, hairless but rough, white to pink; lobes erect, short, rounded. **ANTHERS** 4, ±completely protruding, rough and *spurred at the base*. **STYLE** protruding; stigma club-shaped.

This species was previously known as *Blaeria equisetifolia*.

J F M A M J J A S O N D

Erica longimontana

Common along the southern slopes of the Langeberg from Swellendam to the western Outeniqua Mtns

FORM Upright, closely branched shrublet to 70cm, with numerous flowering branchlets bearing many closely packed short-shoots. **LEAVES** 3-whorled, needle-like, *hairy with a mix of velvety and usually long wispy hairs*. **FLOWERS** in 2- to 6- flowered clusters at the tips of the branchlets and short-shoots, aggregated into false-racemes, stalked; *bracteoles near the base of the flower stalks*, scale-like, hairy. **SEPALS** needle-like, *hairy* with a mix of velvety and usually also long wispy or whisker-like hairs. **COROLLA** urn-shaped or narrowly funnel-shaped and 4-ribbed or 4-angled in the lower half, 2.5–4mm long, rough and velvety or sometimes hairless, dark or reddish pink; lobes erect, blunt. **ANTHERS** 4, fully or mostly protruding, rough with *long, minutely barbed tails* at the base. **STYLE** protruding; stigma club-shaped.

This species was previously known as *Blaeria coccinea*.

J F M A M J J A S O N D

Cluster 2 ▪ NUT-FRUITED HEATHS

Fruit woody but not splitting open to release the seeds, 2- to 4-chambered with 1 seed per chamber; sepals separate to the base. (These species were previously placed in the genera *Acrostemon* and *Thoracosperma*.)

Erica rosacea

Rosy Heath

Rocky slopes, sometimes dominant; southern coastal and inland mountains from Swellendam and Touws River to Humansdorp

FORM Upright or sprawling shrublet to 1m, with numerous flowering branchlets.
LEAVES 3-whorled, needle-like. **FLOWERS** in 1 to 3 whorls near the tips of the branchlets, on short stalks; bracteoles pressed against the calyx, needle-like, red. **SEPALS** red or greenish.
COROLLA 4-lobed, tubular or urn-shaped, 2–4mm long, hairless, pink; lobes erect, rounded.

> This species was previously known as *Thoracosperma rosacea*.

| J | F | M | A | M | J | J | A | S | O | N | D |

ANTHERS 4, protruding, *spurred at the base* with the *spurs usually partly joined to the filaments*. **OVARY** *mostly 4-chambered*. **STYLE** protruding; stigma obscure. **FRUIT** not splitting open, woody.

Nicky van Berkel

Erica eriocephala
Woolly-headed Heath, Rosemary Heath

Porterville along the coastal ranges to Kleinmond and from Tulbagh inland to Robertson

FORM Low, upright or sprawling shrublet to 40cm, with numerous flowering branchlets. **LEAVES** (3)4-whorled, needle-like, hairless or covered with bristle-like hairs. **FLOWERS** in a head or short raceme at the tips of the branchlets and also on highly reduced spur-shoots in the upper axils, on short stalks or stalkless; bracteoles ±pressed against the calyx, needle-like in lower flowers but minute and scale-like like in upper flowers, softly hairy. **SEPALS** needle-like and grooved, *densely silky with long white hairs, reddish*. **COROLLA** *shortly tubular or egg-shaped, slightly swollen* and *4-angled* at the base, closed at the tip, 2–3mm long, pink; lobes small and almost closing the mouth, blunt. **ANTHERS** 4, fully protruding, *rounded at the base*. **OVARY** *2- or 3-chambered*. **STYLE** protruding; stigma obscure or pinhead. **FRUIT** not, or partly, splitting open, woody.

| J | F | M | A | M | J | J | A | S | O | N | D |

This species was previously known as *Acrostemon hirsutus*.

Cluster 3 ■ GRAIN-FRUITED HEATHS

Fruits thin-walled and not splitting open to release the seeds, 1- or 2-chambered with 1 seed in each chamber; sepals usually joined in a cup-like or tubular calyx. (These species were previously placed in the genera *Anomalanthus*, *Grisebachia*, *Simocheilus*, *Sympieza* and *Syndesmanthus*.)

Erica uberiflora

Multi-flowered Heath

Common on rocky slopes and sandy flats throughout the southern coastal and inland mountains but also in the southern Cederberg

FORM Upright, slender or compact shrublet to 1.5m, with numerous flowering branchlets bearing short-shoots. **LEAVES** 3-whorled, needle-like, hairless or hairy. **FLOWERS** in 1 to 4 whorls congested into a nodding cluster at the tips of the branchlets and the short-shoots, which are often clustered into false-racemes, stalkless; *bracteoles pressed against the calyx*, needle-like or scale-like, pink. **SEPALS** *joined in a 4-lobed, tubular calyx* with a *deep longitudinal groove in line with the gaps between the lobes*, hairless or hairy along the grooves, pink. **COROLLA** tubular and narrowed below, 3–4mm long, hairless, pink or rarely white; lobes erect, rounded. **ANTHERS** 4, completely protruding, *tailed at the base*. **OVARY** 2-chambered. **STYLE** protruding; stigma obscure or slightly cup-shaped. **FRUIT** not splitting open, papery.

> This species was previously known as *Simocheilus barbiger*.

| J | F | M | A | M | J | J | A | S | O | N | D |

Erica glabella

Ribbed Heath

Dry rocky slopes on the Cape Peninsula and Hottentots Holland Mtns along the Kleinrivier Mtns to Breede River Mouth

FORM Upright or sprawling shrublet to 50cm, with numerous flowering branchlets. **LEAVES** *(3)4-whorled*, needle-like, hairless or hairy. **FLOWERS** in 4 to 6 whorls congested into a nodding head at the tips of the branchlets, stalkless; *bracteoles absent or rarely present in the lower flowers*. **SEPALS** *joined in a 4-lobed, cup-like calyx* with a *longitudinal rib in line with each calyx lobe*, hairless or hairy. **COROLLA** tubular and narrowed below, 3–5mm long, hairless and smooth or rough and sandpaper-like, pink; lobes obscure, erect, rounded. **ANTHERS** 4, completely protruding, rounded at the base. **OVARY** mostly 2-chambered. **STYLE** protruding; stigma obscure. **FRUIT** not splitting open, papery.

> This species was previously known as *Simocheilus glabellus*.

J	F	M	A	M	J	J	A	S	O	N	D

Ross Turner

Erica labialis

Common in the extreme southwest of the Cape Peninsula and from Tulbagh to the Kogelberg and along the Kleinrivier Mtns to Elim

FORM Upright, compact shrublet to 80cm, with additional flowering branchlets.
LEAVES 3-whorled, needle-like, hairless or hairy. **FLOWERS** in 4 to 9 whorls congested into a nodding head at the tips of the branchlets, stalkless; bracteoles absent or rarely present in the lower flowers. **SEPALS** *of lower flowers in each head joined in a broad, flattened, 2-lobed calyx*; upper flowers with 4-toothed tubular calyx, hairless or hairy. **COROLLA** 2-lobed, tubular or funnel-shaped and narrowed below, 2.5–7.5mm long, hairless but rough, pink; lobes erect, rounded. **ANTHERS** 4, completely protruding, rounded at the base. **OVARY** 2-chambered. **STYLE** protruding; stigma obscure. **FRUIT** not splitting open, papery.

Ross Turner

> This species was previously known as *Sympieza labialis*.

| J | F | M | A | M | J | J | A | S | O | N | D |

Erica similis

Darling to the Cape Peninsula, eastwards to near George

FORM Upright or sprawling shrublet to 50cm, with additional flowering branchlets.
LEAVES *4-whorled*, needle-like, hairless or hairy. **FLOWERS** in up to 6 whorls congested into a nodding head at the tips of the branchlets, stalkless; bracteoles absent. **SEPALS** *joined in a 4-lobed, tubular calyx* with a *thickened longitudinal rib in line with each lobe*, hairless or hairy on the ridges and with long wispy hairs along the margins. **COROLLA** tubular or funnel-shaped and narrowed below, 2.5–4mm long, hairless, pink; lobes erect, rounded.
ANTHERS 4, completely protruding, rounded at the base. **OVARY** *1-chambered*.
STYLE protruding; stigma obscure.
FRUIT not splitting open, papery.

> This species was previously known as *Syndesmanthus articulatus*.

| J | F | M | A | M | J | J | A | S | O | N | D |

SIMILAR SPECIES Erica erina from the mountains above Stanford is very similar but the disc-like stigma has a peculiar, finger-like extension in the centre.

Sally Adams

Erica plumosa

Largely a western species, on sandy flats from Nieuwoudtville and Calvinia to the Cape Flats and through the Breede River Valley to Swellendam

FORM Compact shrublet to 1m, with numerous flowering branchlets. **LEAVES** 3(4)-whorled, needle-like, velvety or hairless but *always fringed on the margins with hairs* that are short or long, unbranched or feathery and sometimes gland-tipped. **FLOWERS** in 1 to 3 whorls clustered in small erect or nodding heads at the tips of the branchlets, stalkless or on short stalks; *bracteoles ±pressed against the calyx*, lance-shaped and *usually with pink flattened base, variably hairy*. **SEPALS** separate or joined in a cup-shaped calyx, *often densely covered with long, feathery hairs, pink*. **COROLLA** urn-shaped with a swollen base and constricted throat, 3–4(–7)mm long, *minutely hairy around the neck*, pink; lobes suberect, rounded. **ANTHERS** 4, partly protruding, the lobes short and diverging, *spurred from near the middle*. **OVARY** 2-chambered. **STYLE** protruding; stigma obscure or pinhead. **FRUIT** not splitting open, papery.

> This species was previously known as *Grisebachia incana*.

J	F	M	A	M	J	J	A	S	O	N	D

Erica inaequalis

Dry rocky slopes and sandy flats; a western mountain species from the Kamiesberg and Nieuwoudtville to Worcester

FORM Upright or sprawling shrublet to 40cm, with numerous short-shoots. **LEAVES** 3-whorled, needle-like, hairless or minutely hairy. **FLOWERS** in 1 or 2 whorls at the tips of the short-shoots, aggregated into false-racemes, stalkless; bracteoles needle-like, hairless or minutely hairy. **SEPALS** *joined in a 4-lobed calyx that enlarges and becomes succulent in fruit*, hairless or minutely hairy, pink to red. **COROLLA** tubular and tapering at the base, 3–4mm long, pink to whitish, hairless; lobes erect, rounded. **ANTHERS** 4, completely protruding, rounded at the base but with a minute tooth halfway up each side. **OVARY** 2-chambered. **STYLE** protruding; stigma obscure. **FRUIT** not, or only partially, splitting open, papery.

> This species was previously known as *Simocheilus glaber*.

J F M A M J J A S O N D

Erica anguliger

Widely distributed on dry rocky slopes and sandy flats throughout the southwest and south from Tulbagh to the Kogelberg, eastwards along the coast and inland to Willowmore

FORM Compact or spreading shrublet to 30cm, with numerous branchlets bearing short-shoots. **LEAVES** 3-whorled, needle-like, hairless or minutely hairy. **FLOWERS** mostly in 3s at the tips of the short-shoots along the branchlets, aggregated into dense false-racemes, ±stalkless; bracteoles scale-like. **SEPALS** joined in a 4-lobed calyx, *fleshy when fresh and greatly enlarging in fruit to envelop the corolla, yellow or red becoming woody and black*, hairless or minutely hairy. **COROLLA** bell-shaped and narrowed at the base, 1.5–4mm long, hairless or rarely minutely hairy, rough, pink; lobes erect, rounded. **ANTHERS** 4, completely protruding, rounded or spurred at the base. **OVARY** *1-chambered*. **STYLE** protruding; stigma obscure or cup-shaped. **FRUIT** *hidden within the swollen, berry-like calyx*, not splitting open, papery.

> This species now includes all plants that were previously placed in the genus *Anomalanthus*. The drupe-like fruits enveloped by the swollen calyx are diagnostic.

J | F | M | A | M | J | J | A | S | O | N | D

Sandra Falanga

Carina Lochner

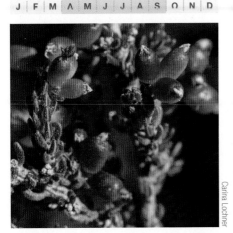

Carina Lochner

Carina Lochner

GLOSSARY

anther sac-like structure containing pollen grains, at the end of the stamen, usually on a slender filament

axil upper angle between a stem and an attached leaf or branch

bract leaf-like organ subtending a flower or inflorescence

bracteole small, second-order bract

calyx collective sepals of a flower, usually leaf-like, protecting the bud

coppice to resprout from near the base of the stem

corolla collective petals of a flower, usually colourful and serving to attract pollinators

cuticle outermost waxy coating protecting a leaf from desiccation

drupe single-seeded fruit with a fleshy or leathery coat surrounding a hard inner shell containing the embryo

ericoid pertaining to small, stiff, needle-like leaves with the margins rolled under, as in many *Erica* species

exserted protruding beyond the surrounding organs, as in stamens protruding from the corolla tube

false-spike narrow, unbranched inflorescence resembling a spike in having a solitary flower in each bract axil borne close to the stem

filament stalk bearing the anther

hybrid individual arising from interbreeding between two different species

inflorescence collective flowers on a single branch or stem

keeled bearing a median longitudinal ridge, as the keel of a boat

lobe free part of an organ when the lower part is joined to adjacent members

margin edge of leaf, flower or sepal

mycorrhiza symbiotic association of a fungus with the roots of a plant

ovary collective female part of a flower containing the ovules, usually divided into two or more compartments (locules)

ovule individual female organ (egg), which after fertilisation becomes a seed

pedicel individual stalk arising in the axil of a bract and bearing a flower at its tip

petal one segment of the inner sterile whorl of a flower, usually colourful; collectively called a corolla

raceme unbranched inflorescence with a solitary, stalked flower in each bract axil; of indeterminate growth, with new flowers growing from the tip

sepal one segment of the outermost sterile whorl of a flower, usually leaf-like; collectively called a calyx

sessile without a stalk

short-shoot small, highly contracted branch bearing tufts of leaves or flowers

shrub woody plant smaller than a tree and without a single trunk but with several main stems from the base

spur short, horn-like protuberance

spur-shoot *see* short-shoot

stamen male part of the flower, comprises a sac-like anther, containing pollen grains, borne on the end of a slender stalk or filament

stigma terminal portion of the style on which the pollen grains germinate, thus usually moist or sticky

stomata small pores in the surface of a leaf allowing exchange of gas between the interior and the atmosphere; each stoma is flanked by a pair of guard cells that can expand or contract to close or open the stoma

style slender column at the top of the ovary bearing the stigma at its tip where it can make contact with a pollinator

tetrad (pollen tetrad) cluster of four adhering pollen grains, formed by the division of a pollen mother cell

tube tubular portion of calyx or corolla formed by fusion of the individual sepals or petals

vestigial highly reduced or underdeveloped

whorl single series of foliar or floral organs radiating from the same point on the floral axis or stem

REFERENCES

Anon. 2021. *Ericas in the Hangklip Region.* Pringle Bay Fynbos Study Group.

Bolus, H., Guthrie, F. & Brown, N.E. 1905. Ericaceae. In W.T. Thiselton-Dyer (ed), *Flora Capensis* 4(2): 2–418, 1123–1129. Lovell Reeve & Co, London.

Freiberg, M. & Manning, J.C. 2013. *Distribution of Plant Diversity in the Core Cape Floristic Subregion.* South African National Biodiversity Institute, Pretoria.

Manning, J.C. & Goldblatt, P. 2012. *Plants of the Greater Cape Floristic Region 1: The Core Cape Flora.* Strelitzia 29. South African National Biodiversity Institute, Pretoria.

Marloth, H.W.R. 1932. *The Flora of South Africa*, vol. 3. Darter Bros. & Co., Cape Town.

Oliver, E.G.H. 1991. *The Ericoideae (Ericaceae) – A Review.* Contributions from the Bolus Herbarium 13: 158–208. Bolus Herbarium, University of Cape Town, Cape Town.

Oliver, E.G.H. 2000. *Systematics of Ericeae (Ericaceae-Ericoideae): Species with Indehiscent and Partially Dehiscent Fruits.* Contributions from the Bolus Herbarium 19. Bolus Herbarium, University of Cape Town, Cape Town.

Oliver, E.G.H. 2012. Ericaceae. In J.C. Manning & P. Goldblatt, *Plants of the Greater Cape Floristic Region 1: The Core Cape Flora.* Strelitzia 29: 482–511. South African National Biodiversity Institute, Pretoria.

Oliver, I. & Oliver, T. 2000. *Field Guide to the Ericas of the Cape Peninsula.* Protea Atlas Project, National Botanical Institute, Cape Town.

Runcie, J. 1910. 'The Bells of Allah' from *Idylls by Two Oceans.* Cape Times Limited, Cape Town.

Salter, T.M. 1950. Ericaceae Lindl. In R.S. Adamson & T.M. Salter (eds), *Flora of the Cape Peninsula*, pp. 626–662. Juta & Co., Cape Town & Johannesburg.

Schumann, D. & Kirsten, G. 1992. *Ericas of South Africa.* Fernwood Press, Cape Town.

INDEX TO *ERICA* SPECIES

INDEX TO COMMON NAMES

Ross Turner